Life
is an
Attitude

How to Grow Forever Better

Dottie Billington, Ph.D.

"This book is good—very, very good. It offers depth. It's liberating. It's the type of book you will want to read over and over."   **Leola Furman, Ph.D., Assoc. Prof., U. of ND**

"Dottie's passion for life is contagious, and we caught it!"
Gwen Langwell, President, Kirkland Women's Club

"An Inspiration for People of All Ages! It's helping me re-discover and reach for higher ground. I'm also using it with my students, to help them gain self-confidence."
Darryl Goff, Special Education Teacher

"The perfect cookbook for retirees. Every chapter is a recipe to forever improve and grow."
Dave Loge, Retired Business Executive, Scottsdale, AZ

"The format is so inviting–you can pick it up and read snippets here and there. And most importantly, it is helpful and wonderfully sensible and inspiring."
Janet Dreyer, Ph.D., Molecular Biologist and Artist

"I'll be re-reading this powerful book for many years to come."   **Sue Reamer, Ph.D., Health Care Executive, MA**

LIFE IS
AN ATTITUDE:

How to Grow Forever Better

by Dottie Billington, Ph.D.

Lowell Leigh Books
Sammamish, Washington

© 2000, 2001 Dottie Billington, Ph.D.
First printing 2000
Second Edition 2001

Although the author and publisher have made every effort to ensure the accuracy and completeness of information contained in this book, we assume no responsibility for errors, inaccuracies, omissions, or any inconsistency herein. Any slights of people, places, or organizations are unintentional.

Publisher's Cataloging-in-Publication

Billington, Dottie.
   Life is an attitude : how to grow forever
better / by Dottie Billington. -- 2nd ed.
   p. cm.
   Includes index.
   LCCN: 99-94590
   ISBN: 0-9671837-0-7

   1. Self-actualization (Psychology) 2. Attitude
(Psychology) I. Title.

BF637.S4B55 2000   158.1
                QBI00-500135

ATTENTION CORPORATIONS, UNIVERSITIES, COLLEGES, AND PROFESSIONAL ORGANIZATIONS: Quantity discounts are available on bulk purchases of this book for educational purposes. Special books or book excerpts can also be created to fit specific needs. For information, please contact Lowell Leigh Books, 27175 S.E. 27th Street, Sammamish, WA 98075, phone 425-369-1584 or email: LLBooks@AdultGrowth.com

CONTENTS

ACKNOWLEDGMENTS

For your honest helpful feedback, your ideas, your stories, your encouragement, I lovingly thank Sue Reamer, Ph.D., Lee Furman, Ph.D., Rich Appelbaum, Ph.D., Karen Shapiro, Kathy Edwards, Ph.D., Alice Rowe, Ph.D., Bill Dreyer, Ph.D., Dulcy Mahaffy, Helen Billington, David Loge, Virginia Allison, Una Loge, Ron Allison, Rody Rowe, M.Div., George Edwards, Don Peters, Keith Greiner, Ed.S., Susan Osborne, Ph.D., Keith Gunnar, Kinne McCabe, M.D., and Antje Gunnar.

To all the men and women who so graciously agreed to participate in my research, my deep gratitude for sharing your time, your experiences, your ideas.

For your generous input and inspiration, I thank Marie Fielder, Ph.D., Alena Moris, Dick Ferrin, Ph.D., Kathleen Ross, Ph.D., and Bill Wortley.

My gratitude, too, to the impressive Fielding Institute. With unparalleled integrity, you walk your talk.

For years one of my favorite artists has been Richard Kirsten-Daiensai, a man not only superbly talented, but also deeply spiritual. To be able to include your work here is an honor. My loving thanks. And for your delightful art I also thank Janet Dreyer, Ph.D., George Kloss, and Teresa Stieg.

And how can I thank you enough, Maggie Querciagrossa. Your enthusiastic encouragement from the beginning, your reading of every word with always-helpful suggestions—together with laughter and fun—made this whole process sing. This book wouldn't have been the same without you.

To all of my loving and supportive family, big hugs of thanks. Especially to Bill, my wonderful husband, thank you for your ever-enthusiastic support, for your sense of humor that levitates even the grimmest of times, for all our brainstorming walks up the mountain, for reading and rereading every word, for everything.

INTRODUCTION

You may know the feeling. When you learn or experience something that changes your life, you want to share it. The purpose of this book is to share with you exciting research about how you can keep right on growing—and feeling more fulfilled—every day of your life.

It all started when I was forty. With my children stretching toward independence, I felt ready for a new challenge. So back to work I went, back to that fascinating world of business. Like a fledgling eagle finally spreading its wings, at first I hesitated, a little frightened. Then, spying the new world spread out before me, I took off.

Because I loved my work, I thrived. Yet soon a fascinating facet of my clients snared and held my interest. Why, I wondered, do bright and good people react so differently to life and its challenges?

Why do some manage their lives so very effectively? They make good decisions. They get along well with others. They're open and learning and growing and enjoying. They're dynamic and vital and excited.

Yet other, equally good people don't seem to do so well. They appear to be stuck.

I wanted to learn the secrets of the dynamic people— how they got that way and how they keep getting better, no matter their age.

For years I watched and wondered and read until finally, at age fifty and passionately curious, I enrolled in graduate school to study adult development. This is a relatively new field of psychology, for until just a few decades ago, psychologists thought only children grow, reach maturity at about twenty, then remain the same for the rest of their lives.

After earning my master's degree I felt I'd but scratched the surface of this challenging subject, so began work on my Ph.D. For seven years I basked in the world of learning and research and working closely with brilliant, inquiring professors and colleagues. It was the most stimulating, enthralling period of my life. I'd found the path of my heart.

Because few have studied how and why some adults continue to grow while others do not, my research has centered on that question. You'll read about my discoveries and about recent research by others. For instance, to learn how they do it, I interviewed men and women in mid-life who are widely admired as exceptionally vital, ever-growing people. They have in common, I found, highly unusual characteristics and ways of handling life's challenges—techniques and attitudes that all of us can adapt for ourselves. Every story in this book is true, although most names have been changed to respect privacy.

You'll find short concise chapters, each offering a technique or idea for you to ponder and practice. You may want to read through the book once, then go back and reread chapters that resonate with you. Or first go straight to parts that entice you most—whatever works best for you.

As I struggled to make these ideas clear for you, the reader, I was forced to clarify and reexamine my own thinking. That reminded me that growing is not a destination; it is a never-ending journey—for we are all splendidly imperfect.

You already instinctively know much of this material. But it helps to be reminded of it, and to think about it in new ways. Think of this book as a reflective pool for your thoughts and plans about where you want to go with your life, about the person you want to *be* and *become*. And please, have fun with your journey!

PART ONE

Your Time is Now

Your Best Is Yet to Be   *1*

*Your capacities are
trembling to be born.*

—ABRAHAM MASLOW

As we walked together one crisp winter morning, my friend Katie confided—looking a little embarrassed, "You know, sometimes I'm afraid of the years ahead, of the direction I'm going. I see too many people growing narrow and negative, bored and boring. They seem stuck. How do I know I won't get that way?"

Her words stunned me. This dynamic, attractive thirty-seven-year-old with tousled curls and bubbling enthusiasm, who seems to have everything going for her—challenging work, good friends, a loving family—dreads her future? At that moment I realized this book had to be written.

The problem is, we Americans have become obsessed with youth. Terrified of growing older, we stomp—kicking and screaming—into mid-life. Somewhere along the way we've lost the wisdom of the ages—that *each succeeding year can bring experience and wisdom you could not have had earlier. Each year is meant to be the flowering of all that came before.*

The important thing to understand is that the picture of life we grew up with has changed. Instead of looking and feeling old by forty, or sixty, we can expect to remain bumptiously bodacious well into our eighties, even our nineties—if we develop a positive attitude and live a reasonably healthy lifestyle (both of which we now know count more than our genes).

Since the beginning of the twentieth century our life expectancy has grown more than in all the previous twenty centuries. Thus, *we have been given the precious gift of time.*

So, whatever your age—twenty or eighty—make the most of it! Inside you, waiting, lies potential beyond your imagination. Your future years can be a time of transformation, meaning, purpose. You can continue to grow in every way—your mind, your wisdom (of course becoming a guru *does* take time—how many thirty-year-old sages are there?), your relationships, your gifts and abilities, the way you feel about yourself, and yes, even physically.

And you can grow happier: Research tells us we can discover more pleasure each succeeding decade, even as we move into our eighties and beyond. The point is, *you can choose to make the rest of your life your best years ever.* The purpose of this book is to help you do just that.

To Begin

Look for role models, vital men and women who make their mature years a time of transformation and spiritual unfolding—the kind of people you want to emulate. Financier Warren Buffett says he can tell how your life will go by learning who your role models are because *the qualities of people you admire are habits and behaviors you can learn.* In the same way, you can choose *not* to have the qualities of people you do *not* admire.

You can find your role models from among people you know, well-known public figures past or present, or from books, the media, or other sources.

Design Your Future Self

1. Begin by getting out a big pad of paper or better yet, a journal. Here and in chapters to follow, writing will help you process your thoughts and insights.

2. Write a detailed description of the kind of person you would like to be ten years from now. Describe your future personality—how you want to feel about yourself, how you want to interact with other people, how you want to live and love, laugh and play, learn and work, contribute to your world.

3. Reread what you've written. Make any additions or corrections you want. (As you read this book, you'll think of other things you'll want to add.)

4. Finally, list any reasons why you cannot become the person you have described.

You—and Katie—have strengths and abilities trembling to be born. You have potential for growth and pleasure beyond imagination. Use this book to help you discover your wonderfully unique potential.

> *If you can dream it*
> *you can become it.*
> *If you can imagine it*
> *You can achieve it.*

R. Kirsten-Daiensai

12

To Grow or Not to Grow 2

*And the day came when the
risk to remain tight in a bud
was more painful than the risk
it took to blossom.*

—ANAÏS NIN

*People do not grow old.
When they cease to grow,
they become old.*

—RALPH WALDO EMERSON

One cold, snowing winter morning two thousand years
ago, philosopher Lao-Tzu was strolling through the forest.
Suddenly he was startled by loud cracking sounds around
him. Looking up, he watched the heavy snow piling high

13

on strong sturdy branches. At first, unbending, they resisted the increasing weight. But finally they broke. Soon he noticed that the smaller, more flexible branches bent with the snow's weight, allowing it to slide off, then bounced back. It is better, he decided, to bend with change than to resist it.

Why grow? Because resisting change damages our very being. Because, as famed psychologist Abraham Maslow wrote, "Our capacities clamor to be used, and cease their clamor only when they are well used. That is, our capacities are also needs."

What matters most is not so much where we are, but the direction in which we are moving. Think about this for a minute: Everything is continually changing. Mountains wear away, continents drift apart, generations come and go. You are alive because at this moment, throughout your body, old cells are dying off and being replaced. Seven years from now every molecule in your body will have been replaced. Thus, our minds and our bodies are in a continual state of flux—w*e cannot remain exactly as we are.*

We do better when we welcome change and join in the flow of life. As Heraclitus wrote, "All things move and nothing remains still.... You cannot step twice into the same stream."

Choosing to grow may seem like an obvious choice, but it isn't easy for everyone. You probably know people who are continually learning; they are vital, enthusiastic, interest*ed*, and interest*ing*. But you probably also know some who seem to be afraid of change, who resolutely cling to their old ways of thinking and doing because that feels safer to them. They protest, "No, I don't want to change. I just want to stay the same." But wouldn't staying the same in an ever-changing world mean slipping backwards, being left behind?

Choosing to stay the same confines a person to one narrow path where he trudges back and forth, day in, day out. Gradually, the path wears deeper and deeper, finally becoming a rut so deep the person can no longer see out. Thus, he loses contact with the world.

Growing, however, is like walking up a mountain. Walking on a trail through the dense woods at the bottom, you see only your immediate surroundings, the path and trees lining it, maybe a small stream in one spot, a waterfall in another. As you climb a little higher the trees thin out, offering new perspectives as you glimpse the valley below. As you continue upward, your view expands to a 180-degree panorama of surrounding foothills, valley, and in the distance, mountains. Only when you reach the top of the mountain, above the trees, can you see the entire landscape, from deserts in one direction to mountains in another to the sea in another.

And only then can you discern the relationships involved, that the stream is the source of the waterfall. That the mountains block the rainfall—which is the reason you see green forests on one side and desert on the other.

As we grow we progress from simple to complex thinking. When less mature, we see things in isolation—a few trees here, a stream there. As we climb toward fuller maturity we become better able to see the whole picture and to understand complex interrelationships—which is the basis of mature thinking.

Many people choose not to climb to the top of the mountain, for the journey involves energy, risk, and discomfort. But the effort is worth it, for each new view brings to you exhilaration, understanding, and wisdom.

There is no pinnacle in our journey of becoming. There is always more to learn—you can continue to grow as long as you live, to discover the genius, power, and magic that exist in you. For growth is not a destination, but a journey. I love the way Kahlil Gibran put it: "The soul unfolds itself like a lotus of countless petals."

Research tells us that adults who choose to grow:
- remain more vital, dynamic, and fully involved with living,
- become more interested and interesting,
- enjoy better physical and mental health,
- are more mentally flexible,
- are more "juicy",

- are more creative,

- have more alive, satisfying relationships,

- like children, appreciate the simple things in life with awe, pleasure, wonder, and ecstasy—however stale these things have become to other people.

How to begin? You need only take the first step, and then a funny thing happens: One small change triggers others—for change creates its own momentum. And once you commit yourself to growth and adopt even one of the ideas in this book, you'll discover that feeling you are growing is so exhilarating that it becomes addictive.

None of us is finished. We all have some ungrown place with potential for growth. One of the most devastating and damaging things that can happen to anyone is to fail to fulfill his potential. A kind of gnawing emptiness, longing, frustration, and anger takes over when this occurs.

—E. T. HALL, ANTHROPOLOGIST

The Power of You   *3*

*To be free is not to
do what one pleases;
it is to become
master of oneself.*

—ANONYMOUS

Rich was one of my professors in graduate school. He's a wonderful guy, but he'd never paid much attention to fitness. One day, when he was forty-three and feeling old, he went with his son to a Bruce Lee movie. As he watched he suddenly said to himself, "Bruce Lee is so fit for his age; there's no reason why I can't be, too." He took up exercise, started running, then long distance bicycling, and now he is *fit!* He confided, "It gave me self-confidence, a sense of myself as a physical person, that I have the ability to do anything."

As you grow older, you can get better not only physically, like Rich, but in almost every way. The kind of person you become is mostly up to you. You, alone, can decide to replace your old, ineffective habits with new ones that work for you. You, alone, can create your future self. I know this sounds simplistic, but think about it a moment. Isn't it true?

In psychology jargon, healthy vital people have an *internal locus of control* instead of an *external locus of control*. That means, instead of blaming other people or the world out there for your problems, realize that in almost all situations you have—within you—the power to influence the direction of your life. *That is the power of you.*

If you decide you want to keep right on growing, to become more and more interesting—and interested, what is there to prevent you—except yourself? All you need is to decide you are ready and willing to make the effort—and then do it.

Here's how to start:

1. Sit quietly, your journal in your lap. Ask yourself, "In what areas of my life do I want to take control?" Consider your mental, physical, and emotional fitness; your relationships with friends, mate, family; your work—anything in your life that matters. Jot down each idea as it comes to you, brainstorming style (see chapter 25).

2. For each thing you've listed, describe in detail your idea of the optimal scenario, the best possible way for that area of your life to be.

3. Now, write down everything you can do to make each of those best scenarios become your reality.

4. Begin your journey.

The point is, you are master of your self. As Rich can choose to become more fit, you can *choose* to take control of your life.

PART TWO

Discover
Your Best Self

Openness

4

He who thinks he knows,
doesn't know. He who knows
that he doesn't know, knows.

—JOSEPH CAMPBELL

"Men jeer at what they do not understand," wrote Goethe, and how right he was. We all tend to resist ideas that are new to us, for we have a natural need to defend our personal view of the world. We want to climb into our box of safe and familiar ideas, scrunch up tight, and pull the lid shut to keep out notions that challenge ours. We tend to think, *others have myths, but I have the truth.*

Almost every scientific theory considered an *absolute truth* in the early twentieth century has since been found false or incomplete. Life, it turns out, offers few absolutes.

In addition, most of our greatest scientific discoveries have met angry resistance, even Louis Pasteur's history-changing discovery of germs. When he suggested that minuscule, invisible organisms were causing the rampant killer epidemics, he was reviled, mocked, ridiculed. Fellow scientists and the public called him an imbecile. No one would believe that something so miniscule, a germ, could cause such devastation in a big human body.

In 1980 my husband Bill suggested we buy a computer because, he said, it would be useful for both of us. At first I was closed to the idea, thinking it was just another gadget that would end up at a garage sale. Of course, it wasn't long before I wanted my own! Oh, well.

Think of the people you know. You can probably see in them a wide range of openness, from completely closed to new ideas to wide-open passionate curiosity and excitement. Now make a mental list of which ones are growing, vital people and which ones seem stuck.

You can't be dogmatic and wise at the same time.

—PAUL BALTES

The point is, openness is a prerequisite of growth. It's as simple as that. *To grow you must be open to learning new, more effective ways of thinking and doing and being.*

An age-old Zen story tells of the professor who considered himself an expert on all subjects, from history to mathematics. Yet because he knew nothing about Zen, he decided to add that to his scholarly repertoire. One day he went to visit Nan-in, a Zen master who lived in a small cottage just outside the town. The master invited him in and, as was the custom, served tea. He filled the professor's cup to the top, and then kept pouring. The tea overflowed the cup, poured onto the table, and trickled to the floor. The professor watched until he could no longer hold back. "The cup is full! No more will go in!"

"Exactly!" said Nan-in. "Your mind is like this cup. It is so full of your ideas and opinions that there is no room for me to show you Zen!"

I found in my interviews with vital, growing people that all of them are passionately curious, full of childlike excitement, delight, and wonder. Their mental antennae continually rotate—listening, searching, discovering new mysteries of life. Rich the professor, said, "I've read enough of the great thinkers to know they're all grappling with truth, and no one has found the answer. So it's all a journey." People like that don't get old. They keep right on learning and growing—as long as they live.

Here are a few tricks to help you stay open:

- Be mindful of how you react to new ideas. Are you open and curious? Or do you find yourself resisting things that are unfamiliar, new, or different?

- When you feel yourself bristling at something you hear, stop and examine your reaction. Irritation usually signals resistance.

- Remember, to all of us most new ideas, at first, sound ridiculous.

Ya Gotta Be Juicy! 5

To err is human,
but it feels divine.

—MAE WEST

Swans sing before they die
—'twere no bad thing.
Did certain persons die
before they sing?

—SAMUEL TAYLOR COLERIDGE

How often do you take time out from your busy life for just plain fun? How often do you stop to smell freshly mown grass or throw your head back and laugh with delight? Most of us would answer "not often enough."

Inner voices from childhood remind us to work hard, achieve, be good, don't do this, don't do that. Somewhere in my head I can still hear my mother saying, "Don't be so unladylike! Would Mrs. Schultz do that?" Mrs. Schultz was our oh-so-proper next-door neighbor. I remember thinking that Mrs. Schultz didn't seem to have much fun.

Life isn't a dress rehearsal. This is it. You can't go back and do it over. When it's over, it's gone—forever! So if you don't live fully now, when will you?

The point is, *Ya gotta be juicy!* Ya gotta savor life, devour it, relish every minute, feast on every precious experience––with gusto! Enjoy all your senses––luxuriate in that gorgeous sunset, in the sweet smell of a spring morn, in all the sounds of life around you, in every touch, every smile, every loving voice. Laugh till it hurts—so what if you sound a little raucous? Why not lust after a scrumptious meal or a sensuous goblet of ruby red wine or someone you love? Why not feel ignited by love and beauty, music and dance, laughter and fun? Why not pack your life full of bodacious delights?

Of course, you need to use good sense with your juiciness. Be sure not to hurt yourself or others in your reveling. It's healthy to be juicy, and it's healthy to use wisdom to set your limits.

I wonder, if Mrs. Schultz had known how much fun being juicy is, would she have enjoyed life more?

You'll know best how you want to put more fun—more juiciness—into your life. Go ahead, indulge—live life to the hilt!

R. Kirsten-Daiensai

Cut Yourself Some Slack 6

*All you can do is
the best you can do,
and the best has its
own reward.*

—ANONYMOUS

Some of us are our own worst enemies. Are you? How do you talk to yourself? Are you encouraging and kind, patient and understanding? Or do you say things to yourself like, "You dummy, you can't do anything right!"

When I asked my very vital ninety-two-year-old mother-in-law, Helen, her secret, she said, "Don't be critical of others—or yourself. Especially yourself. Picking on yourself is like a woodpecker pecking on a tree; eventually that tree's going to fall over."

Just as constantly berating a child undermines self-esteem and development, berating yourself has the same effect. You're human and sensitive and vulnerable and have self-doubts like the rest of us. You need encouragement and positive feedback as much as children or anyone else. And if you don't give it to yourself, who will?

No matter how hard we try, we will never be perfect. No one can. And when you think about it, how do you define "perfect"? Who has the right to determine that? For instance, has there ever been a perfect parent? We can damage children by too much loving, or too little. If we try too hard to help our children become independent, we risk neglecting them.

If a man is gentle and sensitive, he risks being labeled feminine. If a woman is assertive, she risks being called the "b" word. I see the quest for perfection as resembling a balloon; if we squeeze one part, it bulges out elsewhere.

Trust yourself. You are doing your best and that is a pretty fine way to live your life.

Try this: Think of your self-talk as a way of programming yourself. Remind yourself of your gifts, your special magic, your abilities, your strengths and lovableness. And keep it up; help yourself feel warm and fuzzy about who you are.

I keep a little note on my desk lamp that reads, "When we have done our best, we should await the result in peace." And if all my efforts don't work out well, that's OK. In the process of hitting 718 home runs, Babe Ruth struck out 1,330 times.

Discover Your Goals 7

Without goals, you become
what you were.
With goals, you become
what you wish.

—ANONYMOUS

What is most important to you in your life? Are you spending your time on what matters most? Most of us are not, because we haven't mindfully thought about our priorities, or our goals. Yet until we do, how can we make the most of our time—and our lives?

Here is a goal-setting exercise that works—and it's fun. Try it alone or with friends or family. You'll find that doing it every year (on your birthday perhaps) will help you get—and keep—your life on course.

1. Set aside fifteen to twenty minutes. Sit down with four sheets of paper, a pen or pencil, and a watch or timer.

2. Write on the top of the first sheet, *What are my goals for the rest of my life?* Take two minutes to answer this question. Write any ideas that come into your head; include general, specific, trivial, silly, outrageous, stuff-of-dreams, whatever. You may want to include personal, family, career, social, intellectual, or spiritual goals.

3. Next, take two more minutes to go over your list and make any additions or alterations until you are satisfied.

4. Write on the top of the second sheet, *How would I like to spend my next five years?* Again, take two minutes to list your answers as fast as possible.

5. Take another two minutes to make additions or alterations.

6. To give yourself a different perspective on your goals, write at the top of your third sheet, *If I knew I were to die six months from now, how would I live until then?* As-

sume that everything relating to your death—wills and so forth—has been completed. Again, write your answers as quickly as you can for two minutes.

7. Take another two minutes to go back and make any changes you'd like.

8. Now spend two or more minutes going over all three of your lists. You may find that answers to your second and third list are just a continuation of the first, or that in focusing on shorter time periods you shifted to different goals. There are no right or wrong answers. The purpose is to help you discover what is most important to you in your life.

9. Next, prioritize your list. On your fourth sheet of paper, write at the top, *My three most important goals*. Go over all your lists and choose the three that mean the most to you. If you'd like, number the rest in the order of their importance to you and add them to this list.

Why not take a few minutes right now to try this exercise? When you're done, analyze and think about your answers. For instance, if your six-month list contains an entirely different set of goals than your first two lists, you might want to ask yourself if you're ignoring or putting off your most heartfelt needs. Further, if your present lifestyle prevents your progressing toward your important goals, you may want to make some changes, such as eliminating some activities or restructuring your time.

Use this exercise to be sure you are leading the life that means the most to you. And by repeating this each year, you can periodically adjust your goals to keep the trajectory of your life on course.

Create Your Own Future *8*

We cannot direct the wind,
but we can adjust the sails.

—ANONYMOUS

"You sense the direction your life is heading and if that's not what you want, you have to change something," my friend Karen said. In the four years since her divorce she's cocooned herself in work and family and community activities. But now that her son and daughter have married and moved away she confided, "Men are looking so interesting to me lately; I feel ready to start dating."

"But how? I don't even know how to flirt. I treat all men, even those I'm attracted to, like my three brothers," she laughed. So she decided to learn how to flirt, asking friends for pointers, and observing. Also, she joined a health

41

club and three times a week does aerobics and weight training, taking brisk walks on the other days. To trim down and acquire a healthy glow, she started eating more vegetables and fruits, less meat and high-fat foods. Now in her mid-fifties, she's more radiant and attractive than ever before.

Because her social life still revolves around couples from her old life, Karen began ferreting out new activities where she'll be more likely to meet eligible men. And to her friends she's confiding, "I'm ready to start dating, so if you know any nice single men, I'd love an introduction."

After her first blind date, she was disappointed when he didn't call her. Deciding she had nothing to lose, she called him. "I asked him what about me had turned him off, that I hadn't dated in twenty-five years, and was concerned about what I was or wasn't doing. He laughed and said he was looking for a soul mate, and it wasn't me. We ended up having a far better conversation than when we were out to dinner, when he was so nervous he dropped his fork on the floor." They have now become friends.

Instead of passively waiting and hoping for some magical happening, Karen is proactively doing everything she can think of to achieve her goal of finding a wonderful man, maybe even a soul mate. She realizes creating the future you want means:

- proactively taking charge of your own life—acting instead of merely reacting,

- refusing to settle for a future controlled by others or by chance,

- becoming master instead of victim,

- mindfully deciding what you want to happen and then taking the necessary steps to make it happen.

In my studies of vital, ever-growing people, every one of them consciously thinks about the direction they want their life to move and takes steps to make it happen. I've been impressed with how mindfully they plan almost every part of their lives, including relationships, personal growth, physical and mental fitness, their work, even their play. As Marie, a beautiful seventy-four-year-old educator, said, "It's like being in a sailboat. We can let the wind buffet us as it will, or we can use that wind to reach our destination."

In the short term, you're being proactive when, before going into a job interview, you first find out all you can about the company, not only to make sure you want to work for them and that the job will fit your goals, but also to impress the interviewer with your thoroughness. You're being proactive when, before buying a new home or renting an apartment, you first investigate the neighborhood, community, schools, transportation, and everything else that matters to you.

And in the long term, you're being proactive when you figure out how much money you will need to live comfortably when you retire, then set up a savings and investment program to meet that goal. As Warren Buffett said, "Someone's sitting in the shade today because someone planted a tree a long time ago."

Try this:

1. Think of one area of your professional or personal life where you're not fully satisfied.

2. Write down what will probably happen if you make no changes.

3. Next, write down in as much detail as possible the way you would like that part of your life to be, your goal for the best-possible scenario.

4. Sit back and think for a few moments about every possible step you can take to bring about this desired result. Write it all down.

5. Now, make a list of the ways that your passive and proactive end results might differ.

When you live proactively, you create your own future. You adjust your sails to progress in the direction you choose. You plan—and achieve—the kind of life you want. That is *the power of you*.

And then, when you have taken control of your life, don't be surprised when you hear other people say, "There's the one who has all the luck."

R. Kirsten-Daiensai

46

Find Your Passion —and Pursue It

9

Life is a great adventure,
or nothing at all.

—HELEN KELLER

Only she who attempts the absurd
Can achieve the impossible.

—ANONYMOUS

Laura loved her work teaching at a Midwestern university, but chose to forego the writing and research she loved to concentrate on her family. When her husband died she felt lonely, for they'd been married twenty-five years and her sons were away at college. But she was thankful for her work, to which she discovered she could now commit herself, guilt-free.

Eight years later, Laura is radiant! She's passionate about her work—and about life. She's an inspiration to be around and an example of what vintner Robert Mondavi meant when he said, "Interest in something is not enough if you want to excel. You've got to have passion." Now widely recognized for her paradigm-changing research, Laura is continually asked to speak throughout the United States. I've never seen a person grow so much in eight years, and at fifty-six she's still growing!

Laura's passion for life is contagious. To be around her is a joy. When she visits Seattle from the Midwest we don't worry about entertaining her, for she's excited and enthusiastic about whatever we do, whatever she sees, whomever she meets, whatever she eats. (Yes, she's juicy, too.)

One of the best things about mid-life is that finally we have more time to pursue our own passions. How do you find your passion? Gail Sheehy writes, "The more you focus on an activity you like, and the more time you give it, the more likely you are to become passionate about it."

Get involved in something that absorbs you, challenges you, energizes you, makes you feel alive. It could be anything from gardening to writing, from biochemistry to bird-watching. Think about what fascinates you. What subjects do you love to talk about, to read about? What activity do you get lost in? What makes time fly for you?

You might have many passions. Dave, a dynamic fifty-five-year-old corporate executive, said, "My interest spikes at certain things. My passion is finding new challenges that excite me—and new things to learn."

The point is:

- Find what you love to do and do it.
- Never ask yourself if you are good enough to do something—ask only if you love to do it.
- Pursue your passion with all your might.
- What do you have to lose? As Microsoft's President Steve Ballmer says, "Everybody who's any good is a little passionate, aren't they?"

The most powerful force on earth is the human soul on fire. Find your passion—and go for it!

Positive Is Better   10

*You resemble the thought
which you conceive.*

—GOETHE

In 1985 Bill and I went to China with a group of seventeen people. As the weeks went by, we found ourselves feeling more and more irritated by a few people in our group. When alone together we grumbled and grumped about them like a couple of old grinches.

After we got home, we realized our attitude had sullied our trip, admitting, "The problem was us, not them. They were all good people, just being themselves. What earthly right did we have to sit in judgment?" With that *Aha!*, we both felt as if we'd been struck by benevolent lightning. We realized that *when we criticize others, we are not defining them.*

They are already defined. We are defining ourselves, the kind of people we are.

Two years later, as we prepared to travel to Russia, we decided to try a little experiment. We would make a point of trying to discover the special magic in each of our fellow travelers, for by then we realized we truly believe *every person has a special magic all their own*. With our changed attitude, not only was the Russian trip a total delight for us, but there seemed to be an acceptance and appreciation of each other that we'd never before experienced among travel companions. We wondered if a positive accepting attitude is contagious.

We learned you can choose whether you want to be a positive or negative person. And that choice will affect everything in your life—your relationships, your work, how you feel about yourself, and the kind of person you become.

The way you think, positively or negatively, determines the type of filter through which you view and experience life. When you think positively, you perceive life through a clear bright filter. You can still see problems, but you also see potential, that ray of sun shining through the clouds. Life looks, feels, and *is* just plain better. When you think negatively, a dark cloudy filter distorts everything you see and do. Worst of all, it screens out all the positive aspects of your life.

Every negative thing you think, say, or do damages your spirit; it weighs down your wings and keeps you from flying. Negativity affects you mentally, physically, and spiritually.

Since we all need and want to be liked, it's also important to remember that positive people attract others; negative people are hard to be around.

Even after you've decided to be a positive person, you'll find yourself occasionally backsliding into negative thoughts. We all do.

Try this:
- Be mindful of the way you're thinking. When you catch negative thoughts creeping in, just say *stop* and switch back into your positive mode.

- When you feel weighted down by negative thoughts about problems and worries, and you've done all you can to remedy them, break out of it by visualizing putting those worrisome thoughts into a big black balloon. In your mind's eye, hold it by its string, let it go, and watch it soar up, up, and away. As it floats into the clouds, feel the burden lifting from your mind, body, spirit. (I love this technique—it works so well!)

- Ask someone you trust to provide feedback when you slip into negativity.

Whether you have a positive or negative attitude toward life is a matter of habit. *Positive is better.*

R. Kirsten-Daiensai

Magic Moments 11

*Seize the day. Be glad of life
because it gives you the chance
to love and to work and to play
and to look up at the stars.*

—HENRY VAN DYKE

Do you have enough magic moments in your life? That is, moments when you *forget about past and future concerns and melt into the pure joy and magic of the moment?*

Keith, a nature photographer, confided, "I get a thrill when I look out at our bird feeder and see a mother bird feeding her baby. Being a photographer helps me see beauty everywhere; my eyes are forever scanning for interesting shapes, beautiful lighting, colors, patterns—like ripples on the water. It's about *being there, about paying attention to this very moment*, not about doing. I enjoy giving photography classes because it trains people's eyes to look for beauty. Some of my students get tears in their eyes at the end of the class when they share how it's helped them discover a new level of enjoying life."

As Daphne du Maurier wrote, "Happiness is not a possession to be prized. It is a quality of thought, a state of mind."

To discover your most magic moments:

1. Write down as many answers as you can think of for this question: What things in my life bring me joyful, magic moments?

2. Now prioritize your answers according to which give you the most pleasure.

Are you surprised by your answers? My husband Bill and I were surprised by ours. We both found our greatest joy comes from simple everyday things. I cherish walking through my garden early in the morning with a steaming mug of tea, inspecting vegetables and flowers sparkling with dewdrops. I love shopping for groceries, chatting with the fish lady and the produce man. We both love our evenings curled up in front of the fire, reading. It was a revelation to realize that though I love things like my work and my friends, travel and the theater, my greatest joy comes from quiet, simple, everyday activities.

To have magic moments, it helps to *mindfully pay full attention to whatever you're doing, so you can savor every nuance of your experience*. For you, that could mean enjoying a sunrise—the changing colors, the quiet, the beauty. Or it could mean fully *being with* a person you care about, hearing their words, feeling their feelings, caring.

Try this: Hold a fresh lemon, orange, or apple in your hand. Concentrating fully, notice its color, texture, feel. Smell its scent. Does it feel moist and cool, or warm and smooth? Have you enjoyed this moment?

In the long run, instead of great achievements that make you feel good for a while, it is the simple pleasures that, year in and year out, nourish your soul.

Leave a Trail
of Gladness

Lives of great men all remind us
We can make our lives sublime,
And departing, leave behind us,
Footprints on the sands of time.

—HENRY WADSWORTH LONGFELLOW

Years ago I read a wonderful O. Henry story I've never forgotten: A husband and wife, living in an apartment in New York, went out one morning to run errands. The wife was pleasant and friendly to everyone she met, smiling and complimenting for jobs well done. She left a trail of people feeling better about themselves and about life in general.

The husband did the opposite, complaining and insulting everyone he met. He left a trail of discontent and wounded self-esteem. The surprise ending was that the next morning, when the couple again left to run errands, they changed roles: He left a trail of good feelings; she left hurt and dismay.

That story helped me realize you can choose how you want to behave toward others. *You can choose to leave a trail of gladness*. You need not be a great man or woman to leave your footprints on the sands of time, for every time you help someone feel valuable and special, every time you fluff someone's aura, you leave an indelible mark. Such good is seldom forgotten or lost. It becomes part of a person, part of one's soul.

Look for the opportunity to make someone feel valuable. Don't we all want to feel appreciated? Watch how, when you do a kindness, its effects seem to expand, like a ripple from a pebble thrown into a pond. Even when you make room for a car to enter the freeway in front of you, notice that they, in turn, seem to pass on the favor. Kindness is contagious. Let's spread it around!

*I may only pass through
this life once.
Therefore if there is any
kindness I can give you,
let me do so now, for I may
not pass this way again.*

—GAIL SAYERS

Give Back
13

*It is one of the most Beautiful
compensations of this life that
no man can seriously help another
without helping himself.*

—RALPH WALDO EMERSON

It's easy to get so involved in our own lives we lose touch with the world around us. Yet when we limit ourselves to our narrow personal interests, we also restrict our growth as human beings.

Too often we see middle-aged and older people depicted in the media as takers instead of givers, as engaging in nothing more than self-centered activities. Of course, some are that way, but not all. Ninety-three million Americans serve as volunteers. They lovingly give of themselves—their time, friendship, caring, talents, intelligence. You probably know both types of people. Which ones, do you think, feel a deeper sense of self-worth, self-esteem, and self-respect?

> *The purpose of life is to matter—*
> *to count, to stand for something,*
> *to have it make some difference*
> *that we lived at all.*
>
> —LEO ROSTEN

Not only do people who are contributing to society feel better about themselves, research has found that people at mid-life and beyond who are actively involved in their communities are more healthy—mentally and physically. A major source of health and happiness, it turns out, is feeling engaged in life. We need action and challenge. We want to be in the ball game!

When you get fully involved in the world, you become more interesting to be around, so you attract other interesting people as friends, companions, even mates. It's hard to feel lonely when you're out helping others. Life becomes fuller and richer.

I think about it this way: I didn't come this far in life alone. Family and community, friends and colleagues all played a part. Now, with the gift of time brought by children leaving home and lessening work loads, it's my turn to be there for others. It's time to be a mentor to younger men and women beginning careers and relationships, to be there for my friends and loved ones, to teach English to new immigrants, to contribute to my community—to give back, lovingly.

Try volunteering in whatever you feel deeply about. Children need tutoring with their math or reading. Men, women, boys, and girls in crises need an empathetic listener. Many hospitals, schools, and community service organizations depend heavily on volunteer help. You might choose to help out in one of the arts that interests you, such as in a local art museum, in the theater, or with a musical organization. Or you can work with hospice, food banks, big sisters or brothers, or be a mentor to someone looking for guidance. You could volunteer with the Red Cross; they will train you and send you to help out at natural disasters, paying transportation and costs.

Or you could look around you to find a place where help is needed. One morning Joe, the owner of a small auto repair shop in Vermont, was talking with friends at the local coffee shop. One of his buddies told about a young mother trying desperately to get off welfare. Community services helped her get job training, coached her to do well in interviews, then steered her toward job openings. But because there was no public transportation in that area, she had no way to get to an interview—or to work, for she had no car. Joe spread the word that he'd take in unwanted, nonrunning cars. He repaired them and donated them to people needing transportation in order to work. Joe found a need—and filled it.

Susan, who's fifty-four, teaches English as second language to recent immigrants. In small groups of eight to ten adults, she provides a safe environment where these motivated men and women can practice speaking and understanding their new language. "I can see my students speaking better English, getting a little more savvy, showing their sense of humor. You can actually see them becoming less stressed and more sure of themselves. And one by one they come to class to tell us they now were able to get a job. That's payback! And I learn so much about other cultures and people, how to teach better, how to be a better listener. It's a good mental challenge to plan interesting classes and even to sense when a class isn't going well, then to analyze what's wrong and how to improve it. I feel less selfish now."

John, a fifty-seven-year-old architect, started working with hospice patients thirteen years ago. "I've always felt I get more out of it than my patients. I like them as well as anyone I've ever met, and yet, when they die, I feel no grief, because it's their time. It's helped me understand about the inevitability of death—that it's a part of life, a part of living. I realize that just because someone is dying, it doesn't change their personality. A few were kind of nasty people, and you feel a little worse for them when they're dying, because you think they probably never were happy or got much out of life. And I had a few patients who accepted dying and were just wonderful until they died. It gave me a sense of the value of being a decent person, because when you die you leave a legacy. Your family is going to remember you that way instead of thinking, 'The old goat finally died.' I've felt so different about myself in the last thirteen years. I'm very happy."

We're on this earth together—none of us is an island—and we need each other. We cannot seriously help another without helping ourselves, without giving our existence a more deep and abiding meaning. Just look around you, and you'll find a way to give back, a way that fits your gifts.

Begin With Today

14

When the tide of life turns
against you, and the current
upsets your boat, don't waste
tears on what might have been,
just lie on your back and float.

—ANONYMOUS

Ever look back and wish you'd done some things differently? I wish I had been a more nurturing mother. My husband and I wish we'd bought Microsoft stock ten years ago. It's easy to suffer about what you could have done, moaning, "If only I'd done this...or that."

But think about it. Most of us are the best parents, at the time, that we know how to be. Most of us try to make the best possible decisions about our love or work or investments. The point is, we should never be ashamed of saying we know now we could have done better, or we were wrong, for that admission also says we are wiser today than we were yesterday. And how much better can we do than that?

We've all made mistakes. Good old hindsight! We can't undo the past. The only advantage in looking back is to learn to do better in the future.

Let's say you bought a hundred shares of a hot stock five years ago at fifteen dollars a share. Today, after steadily sliding, it's worth only three dollars a share. The price you paid is irrelevant. Today that money is gone, irretrievable. It wastes your emotional energy to fret and suffer over what happened long ago. You made your best decision at the time. *Begin with today:* What you now have is an investment worth three hundred dollars—period! Make your decision based on today's reality.

The same principle holds for relationships, jobs, or wherever you have invested time, energy, or money. If the job you've had for nine years leaves you feeling bored and you're getting nowhere, why not think about making a change? If you were unemployed, would you choose the job you have now? Making the decision to stay, even if you've already invested nine years, is essentially doing just that. Take a fresh look at *today's* options.

It's like paying two hundred dollars for a class you don't like and are getting nothing out of. You may think, "If I quit, I lose all that money." But if you don't quit, that money is still gone and you've lost your time, too.

The point is, *Begin with today. You can't change the past. You can only change the future, and since you are wiser now, start today to create the future you want.*

PART THREE

Your Winning Attitude

Be Happy
All life
Some sun
Some rain.

R. Kirsten-Daiensai

R. Kirsten-Daiensai

Decide to Be Happy 15

Happiness is not a goal,
it's a way of traveling.

—WILLIAM JAMES

"It's your mental attitude, that's all there is to it," says Helen, my mother-in-law. "Every morning I wake up and say, 'It's a new day.' I can't tell what will happen tomorrow and I don't worry about what happened yesterday. If I have negative thoughts I flush them out and substitute constructive ones. *I consciously choose to be up.*"

Study after study reveals that happiness has little to do with age. You will probably be just as happy at seventy or eighty-five as you were at thirty or forty-five. Or more so. Even people permanently disabled in accidents soon bounce back to their former level of happiness. They're like the twisted, gnarled old wind-blown trees on a mountain ridge that endure disease and drought and storms, and emerge stronger and more vital than those protected trees farther down the mountain.

The point is, people who have enjoyed easy lives, who have endured few disasters, suffering, or loss, tend to be less strong or resilient emotionally. Adversity, if not overwhelming, builds strength and character.

Helen had polio as a child and depends on her electric three-wheeled scooter to get around. A widow, she lives alone on a limited income. A happy life? To Helen, life is fascinating and full of pleasure. And what a joy she is to be around!

Keys to a happy attitude:
- Decide to be happy. To a certain extent you create your own happiness—from the inside out.
- Happiness can survive the loss, suffering, and grief that are part of all our lives, and make us stronger. What

matters most is not what happens to you, but how you react.

- Since no life can always be happy, when sometimes you feel miserable it helps to remember, *this too shall change*.

- True happiness consists of getting out of yourself, of focusing your attention on the world instead of on yourself. That means having an active life and absorbing interests.

- Test your known and *yet-to-be-discovered* skills through some meaningful activity. Anything that challenges you will work.

- Genuinely care about other people.

- Make it a habit to consciously remind yourself every day of things for which you are thankful.

> *Most people are just about as happy as they decide to be.*
>
> —ABRAHAM LINCOLN

Generosity of Spirit 16

*Wisdom comes more
from understanding
than from knowledge.*

—ANONYMOUS

When my friend Evelyn said a life goal for her has been to develop generosity of spirit, that clicked with me. I asked what it meant, and she answered, "To me it means filling out those places in me that could be more gentle and accepting, more loving and patient. It means instead of finding peoples' faults, finding their magic."

It means that when a store clerk is unpleasant, instead of reacting angrily, realize she probably has a reason. Maybe her last customer was rude to her or she's worried about a sick child.

It means that when someone cuts you off on the freeway, assume they didn't mean to and let it go. The other day I was chatting with the owner of our health club, Arnie, a burly thirty-nine-year-old bodybuilder. He told me he thought he'd done a lot of growing up in the last few years, especially since marrying Lynn, a gentle loving woman. He said, "The biggest change came one day as I was driving down the freeway. A car cut in too close and I sped around him and made a rude gesture. Then I looked at him. He was an elderly man, and he looked right at me with this look of absolute terror on his face and tears were rolling down his cheeks. I felt so terrible. I've never forgotten. Look at my arm; every time I think about that I get goose bumps all over." Arnie's face actually looked stricken and I saw that his arm, resting on the treadmill was, indeed, covered with goose bumps.

A guiding principle for Helen is, "Be generous and kind and thoughtful to everyone. We have to live together—that's all there is to it."

Generosity of spirit means realizing that most people are doing their best and usually there's a good explanation for their behavior.

It's remembering that we're all different. No two of us see life exactly the same way, so no two of us react the same way. So what right have I to judge or criticize others?

Roger, a friend who is an insurance executive, tells about taking a philosophy class where the assignment was to read selected passages from Plato, Nietzsche, the Bible, *Bhagavad Gita*, "and other guys I'd never been exposed to, being an engineering major in college." The group was then asked to share their understanding of what the authors were saying.

"Generally, out of eight people, all reasonably intelligent and well-educated, there would come three or four widely divergent interpretations and spirited, sometimes heated, discussions. Like, 'Really, it's very clear. How could you possibly see it any other way?' But gradually, with some wise intervention by the professor, most of us began to accept the reality that things do not have to be black or white, right or wrong. Diverse opinions can and do coexist."

Of the three basic tenets of Confucianism, the first is *jen*, which simply means human-heartedness. Isn't it interesting that this philosophy, which has guided a large portion of the world's population for over twenty-five hundred years, is largely based on the simple concepts of love, goodness, and caring?

As you move through life, at some point you reach a fork in the road and have the opportunity to choose the direction you want to go. Generosity of spirit defines the high road. When you hear yourself thinking critical or negative or angry thoughts, why not adjust your direction by asking yourself, "What about generosity of spirit?"

Let Go of the Kids   *17*

*Three older women were sitting
on a park bench. One groaned.
Her friend, sitting next to her,
gave a sigh. The third looked
at both of them and said,
I thought we weren't going to
talk about the children.*

—ELLEN J. LANGER, FROM *MINDFULNESS*

Here's a hot tip on extending your life by eight years,
enough time to blow the kids' inheritance with a trip around
the world. All you have to do is balance your involvement
with your grown children with a stimulating life of your
own.

Studies here and in Europe reveal that parents who are fully involved in their own active, independent lives instead of living *through* their children live longer, healthier lives. In other words, centering your life *primarily* around your children is hazardous to your health as well as to the well-being of your children.

Bill and I tell ourselves that we've already raised our children. We did our best and it's time to stop. We realize that assuming they can't manage their lives without our advice insults them. (Oh, but sometimes withholding advice is so hard!) One of the reasons I loved my in-laws so much is that they never once gave us advice unless we asked for it. However, my mother-in-law Helen now confesses, with a twinkle, "But we really had to bite our tongues sometimes to keep quiet."

It's a tough balancing act to maintain a close, loving, involved relationship with your children while remaining discreetly detached. You probably will agree that it's especially challenging to be a good listener without prying or offering unasked-for advice.

"But," said friends Rich, a professor, and Karen, an artist, "we're close to our kids. We talk by phone all the time. It doesn't feel right to detach now. All four are still in their twenties, single, and just getting started in their careers. Don't they need our support?" We all agreed that children of any age benefit from supportive parents—that what matters is Rich and Karen are passionately pursuing challenging, satisfying lives of their own. They're neither living through nor focusing their lives upon their children.

Grown kids can be stressful. You've survived the ups and downs of your life and probably grew because of the hardest parts. *What doesn't kill you makes you grow.* You don't need to go through all that again with your kids. They may even get divorced or lose jobs or have mid-life crises, and they'll hurt and you'll hurt for them. We can't prevent life from happening to our children, and it would damage everyone concerned if we did. Love them, care about them and sympathize with them, but let them live their own lives, for *love also means letting go.*

You invested years of your life in your children. Now is the time to find new purpose, new goals in your own life. Find people and things that excite you, pursuits where you can focus your time, energy, sense of self, intelligence, and enthusiasm! Now is the time for you to spread your own wings—and soar.

You Can Always Be Attractive

18

Exuberance is Beauty.

—WILLIAM BLAKE

My friend Rose Ann's twenty-eight-year-old son, a golf pro, works with men and women of all ages, from very young to very old. One day she was fretting to him about getting older and worrying about losing her looks. He said, "Mom, a woman is good looking to me at any age, as long as she's good-natured, has a sharp-looking haircut, and looks fit."

To me, the same goes for men. The point is, you can always be attractive. We tend to add pounds as we add years, but that's not all bad. If you get too thin, your face looks older. The trick is to let yourself add just enough weight to keep your face and body looking their best.

Above all, aim for optimal fitness. Tall, proud posture announces vigor and vitality. There's nothing as attractive as the physical and psychological exuberance that comes from good old physical exercise.

Plastic surgery? If a little sagging bothers you, why not get a tuck here and there if finances allow. Color your hair? If it makes you look and feel better, why not? There's a healthy side to vanity (one symptom of depression is not caring how we look). Our self-image is part of who we are. Wanting to reach our full potential, in every realm, is a mark of a healthy, vigorous adult.

But, *the big difference in how you look comes from what's inside*. If you're doing interesting things, exercising, eating right, nurturing your relationships, thinking positively, and feeling good about yourself, you'll look wonderful.

Try this:

- Jot down the names of mature people you know, or have observed, who are still wonderfully attractive.

- Now jot down names of those who have not retained their attractiveness (you may want to exclude those who have suffered a debilitating illness or tragedy).

Next to each name, make a check mark if:

1. They exercise regularly.

2. They conscientiously control their weight.

3. They eat a healthy, well-balanced diet.

4. They are positive thinkers.

5. They truly care about other people.

6. They give back to their community.

7. They value and work on having good relationships.

8. They keep their minds active and stimulated through a variety of interests and activities.

9. They are good-natured.

Now, compare which names have the most check marks. Do you see any patterns emerging? Can you think of any other differences between the two lists that are not included above?

As we mature, our physical features recede in importance in determining our attractiveness. What takes precedence is the kind of person we are and how we choose to live our lives.

By conducting yourself beautifully, you exude beauty.

—ANONYMOUS

You Can Choose How to React

19

*God, grant me the serenity to accept
the things that I cannot change,
the courage to change the things that I can,
and the wisdom to know the difference.*

—THE SERENITY PRAYER

Have you ever, when faced with a crisis that left you spinning emotionally, reacted inappropriately and been sorry later? Most of us know that feeling. But we can *learn* to react more effectively. Even in the worst of situations, *we can choose how we want to react*.

After years of saving and planning, our neighbors Sue and Russ finally built their dream home and settled in with delight. One Saturday morning a few months later they went for a walk in the mountains. They returned home to the low rumbling roar of cascading water that "sounded like a waterfall." Stunned, they splashed in through ankle-deep water to find torrents gushing through ceilings—furniture, rugs, family pictures drenched—and upstairs a geyser spurting from a broken pipe.

Sue looked at Russ, took a deep breath, and said, "OK, honey. We have a choice. Nobody's hurt. We have insurance. We can let this devastate us, or we can do what needs to be done and consider it a challenge." They did just that, and actually enjoyed having good-natured workmen around—and eating out—while the house was torn up.

Friends and neighbors couldn't understand such calmness amidst devastation and chaos. But think about it: Sue and Russ knew they could choose how to react. What choice makes the most sense to you?

You can let a bad situation overwhelm and embitter you, or you can decide what must be done, do it, and get on with your life.

Try this:

1. Visualize yourself reacting the way *you wish* you had to your last stressful situation. Could this different choice

have been more effective?

2. Next time, and every time a difficult situation or crisis arises, think to yourself that you can *choose* how you want to react. When you feel that inevitable rush of emotion, catch yourself and consciously shift into a rational mode by asking, "What is the most effective and positive way for me to react?"

You're human, so there will still be times when you'll look back and realize you could have reacted more effectively. But when you're mindful of the *power of you*, you will learn with each experience. Soon you'll find that *deciding* to react with equanimity acts as a self-fulfilling prophecy, for you'll have *programmed* yourself to automatically slip into a rational, calm mode. Then, almost miraculously, you'll find your problem situations deflating.

The key is to remember that *you alone* control how you react. You can decide to let the challenges in your life overwhelm you, or to use them as stepping stones toward growth.

> *No victory is as great as*
> *becoming master of yourself.*

R. Kirsten-Daiensai

Beyond Conformity *20*

*We do not fulfill our destiny
by imitating others.*

—ANONYMOUS

For most of us, our passionate goal during adolescence was to be accepted and to impress others. We had to wear the "right" clothes and do the "in" things so the other kids would think we were cool, or even just OK.

And even now, as you move into mid-life and beyond, do you still feel a little pressure to conform? Do you sometimes feel as if friends, family, work, church, or community press you to think, dress, and act *their* way, leaving you feeling a little uncomfortable about being purely yourself?

Yet to continue our journey toward full maturity we must move beyond conformity to the post-conformity of self-actualizing adults. We do not fulfill our destiny by imitating others. Maturity happens only when satisfying our own self-set standards becomes more important than reputation, appearance, status, or impressing others. Maturity means shifting from basing our ideas of truth upon what the "authorities" say to looking carefully at a variety of viewpoints and then forming our own. It means dropping our masks, our pretenses, our false pride. It means becoming authentically, uniquely, purely ourselves.

My husband Bill went through a period when all his friends and colleagues were dedicated golfers. He tried it for a while, but couldn't work up any enthusiasm and soon found himself dreading his weekly golf games, wishing he could use the time to do the things he really loved, like hiking in the mountains or catching up on his reading. Finally, realizing he wasn't being true to himself, that he was doing it just to fit in, to please others, he quit.

As Kierkegaard, the Danish philosopher wrote, "The most common despair is...not choosing, or willing, to be oneself.... The deepest form of despair is to choose to be another than oneself."

Take a moment to think about this: Your fingerprints and genes, personality and mind, abilities and interests are *yours alone*. No one else on earth comes close to duplicating you. You are unique. You are special. And that is a treasure for you to cherish—and protect. You were meant to do one thing in life—to become your authentic self.

To become fully yourself, do not follow in the path of another. Use the wisdom of your body, mind, and spirit to find and follow your own path.

Most of us have been brought up to conform and fit in. And in one way, of course, that's necessary; a harmonious society requires its citizens to follow certain laws and standards of decency and consideration. In most areas of life, such as work, family, and community, we need to conform in some ways for things to go smoothly. But at that point the advantage of conforming stops.

- Be yourself, for that is where your magic lies.

- Let your own style shine through!

- Peel away your need to conform and allow the real you to emerge—radiantly.

In her study of vital women in their seventies and eighties, Cecile Hurwich found that nine out of ten said *they are happier now than at any time in their lives.* Hurwich found that every one of these vital women marches to her own drummer, refusing to conform to society's brain-numbing stereotype of how older women should behave. Now *there* is something to think about!

Another thing to think about: If you choose to conform, who will you copy? If most of the middle-aged men and women in the United States have high blood pressure, should you too? In other words, if we decide to conform, isn't it a good idea to be mindful of who and what we're conforming to?

We are all heretics to someone. Everyone doesn't have to approve of you. None of us has 100% approval from everyone. The main thing is to win your own approval, to be fully yourself and to like who you are—a radiantly unique individual. And if not now, when?

Each of us
Exists
To carry out a special mission
A Task
That Belongs
To no other.

—R. KIRSTEN-DAIENSAI

Go With the Flow   *21*

R. Kirsten-Daiensai

*When it starts
to rain, let it.*

—ANONYMOUS

Years ago, we took our nine-year-old son Mark for a walk in the mountains. After stopping for a picnic beside a rushing rocky stream, Bill and I relaxed as Mark played nearby. Suddenly we saw him hurtling, on his back, down the churning current. Horrified, we rushed to save him, sure he'd crash into a rock. But as we reached the bank we saw him happily, serenely, like a floating leaf, gliding along with the flow, easing around the rocks, never into them. Soon he climbed out and, chortling happily, trotted uphill to repeat his adventure.

For me, that experience became a metaphor for living: Whenever I start to fume and fuss about something, I visualize relaxing and flowing gently around the rocks, around my problems.

For example, you've probably known people at work or relatives who at times become contentious, critical, controlling—just hard to be around. It doesn't help to try to placate or reason with them; you can't change them. What you can do is let go, relax, and flow around them, trying to stay out of their way—if not physically, at least mentally and emotionally (see chapter 24).

To go with the flow, let go of negative feelings—anger, fear, guilt, envy—any of those dark brooding thoughts and emotions that eat away at you, sapping your strength and well-being. Sometimes I catch myself dwelling on negative experiences, excusing myself by thinking, "I need to process this thing." But if I "process" too long, I remind myself to shift back, to flow around the negatives and back into positive, constructive thinking.

Teresa, a psychotherapist, and Ben, a cardiologist, had turned their home into a battleground, especially around election time. Both strong and determined—she a Democrat, he a Republican—they fought over every candidate and every issue. One morning after a particularly heated battle, Ben stomped off to work and Teresa was in the shower, consumed by anger, ferociously scrubbing her hair. Suddenly she stopped and said to herself, "I don't want Ben to tell *me* how to think. So what right have I to tell *him* how he should think?" For Teresa, it was an epiphany, a revelation.

Later, she called Ben and arranged to meet him for dinner. Over pasta, by candlelight, she told him what had happened and after they talked it over, he agreed. Enthusiastically. Now both believe that they and their marriage have grown to a new level. And the benefits have spread to every personal interaction in their lives.

Rigidly clinging to *the rightness* of our own ideas, refusing to acknowledge the legitimacy of other people's thinking leads, in essence, to crashing into the rocks. There are few absolute truths in life, and only by remaining mentally flexible and relaxed—letting your mind flow around and through new ways of thinking—can we learn and grow. (And remember, only when we cease to learn do we become old!)

As John Maynard Keynes wrote, "The real difficulty in changing lies not in developing new ideas but in escaping from the old ones."

Can you think of a time when something you've attempted to do just wouldn't work out, no matter how hard you tried? For instance, Lisa and three friends decided to take a winter vacation together in Mexico. After weeks of difficult compromises they finally decided on a date, but then argued over whether they'd go to Cozumel or Mazatlan, and whether they'd stay in a condo or a hotel. Lisa felt as if she was swimming against the current, so gently backed out and asked an old friend to join her on a trip to Hawaii. They had a wonderful time.

Sometimes when a situation doesn't feel right, you may want to redefine your goals, or back off for a while, or look for a more natural direction to flow. Listen to your intuition. Don't push the river. Don't use your energy fighting something that simply isn't working. It may be a sign it's wrong for you.

Try this:

- Close your eyes and think about a problem in your life, something you can't seem to fix. Breathe deeply and visualize yourself letting go, relaxing, flowing gently and easily around your problem. Take a few moments to enjoy a sense of peace and quiet.

- In what other areas of your life would you benefit by relaxing and going with the flow? Jot down any helpful ideas that come to you.

PART FOUR

Habits of Growing Adults

Mindfulness 22

We are what we repeatedly do.
Excellence, then, is not an act
but a habit.

—ANONYMOUS

Twelve-year-old Erik, watching his mother prepare a ham for dinner, noticed that she carefully cut off one end before putting it in the oven. "Why do you cut the end off?" he asked. "Because that's how Grandmother did it," she answered. Later Erik asked Grandmother. She answered, "Because that is how my mother did it." So he went to Great-grandmother, and she explained, "Well, my dear, I always cut off the end of the ham because I didn't have a big enough pan."

This is an example of the opposite of mindfulness, which is mindlessness. *Mindfulness means paying attention to what you are doing and why you are doing it.* It means being aware of the value of standing back and observing yourself objectively and thinking, "Is this the best way?" Or, "Are there other alternatives I should be considering?"

Harvard psychologist Ellen Langer in her book *Mindfulness* tells how mindless behavior caused the 1985 crash of an Air Florida plane. On a freezing-cold day in Washington, D.C., before taking off on a flight to Florida, the pilot and copilot, who were used to flying in warmer climates, went through their routine checklist and, out of habit, checked "off" on the anti-icer. But this time they were flying in freezing weather, and seventy-four people died.

Mindfulness means being fully present in the moment. It means instead of functioning on autopilot, you remain mindful about what you say, and do, and want to accomplish. (Of course, some things we must do automatically, like tying our shoes and other such everyday functions.)

You've probably found yourself drawn into a mindless encounter when someone wants to argue for the sake of arguing. Before you realize what's happening you find yourself engaged in an unpleasant and pointless hassle. It's like the boiled-frog story. When a frog is dropped into cool water and the water is slowly heated to boiling, the frog will remain in the water until it dies. But if the frog is dropped into boiling water, he will hop out immediately. Can you think of a time when you felt boiled because you weren't mindful of what was slowly happening to you?

You'll find that mindfulness will mean different things to you at different times. It is the basic idea of living mindfully, rather than mindlessly, that can help you live your life more effectively.

Try this. Starting now, during your day periodically ask yourself:

- Why am I doing this?

- Is this the best way to do it?

- Is there a different way to do this?

- Am I doing this out of habit?
- Am I being mindful?

Listen to Your Feelings of Dissonance

23

We lie loudest when
we lie to ourselves.

—ERIC HOFFER

While waiting for an elevator in a downtown public building, forty-four-year-old Ron noticed two young men nearby, also waiting. He felt a rush of discomfort but didn't know why. When the elevator came he stood back until the other two got on and then quickly backed away. Later he learned a tourist had been attacked and robbed on one of those elevators.

Listening to his dissonance may have saved Ron's life. When he analyzed why he'd reacted thus, he remembered both men had been wearing long loose raincoats, one was fidgeting in his pocket, and both acted nervous. Our intuition picks up clues that our conscious mind takes longer to process, or may miss altogether.

Pay attention to your vague feelings of discomfort; they are a signal that something in your life is wrong. It's easy and human to deny or ignore signals of problems. We all fool ourselves sometimes, and we're the easiest ones to fool. But denial usually leads to far greater problems.

For years John loved his work as an electronics engineer. He felt challenged, stimulated, and appreciated. But then, at about age forty, his attitude began to sour. He complained, lost enthusiasm, and was sick more often; his work life lost its luster. Finally he decided the problem was that he didn't like the management in his company. So he moved to another. No improvement. After a year of increasing dissatisfaction and stress-related ailments, John decided to take two weeks off to assess his situation. He read career-planning books, talked with a career counselor, and finally realized the problem didn't lie with his company. The problem was that engineering no longer stimulated or excited him. What was right for him at twenty-four no longer fit at forty. He had grown and changed. What he really wanted now was to work independently, to design an environment where he could exercise all of his creative abilities. He quit his job, found a field that called for his unique skills, started his own company, and has worked happily ever since.

In every area of your life uncomfortable feelings can alert you to stand back and take a good objective look:

- Is a relationship going sour?
- At work are you losing interest, getting bad reviews, or dreading each day?
- Are you feeling less vigorous, physically or emotionally?
- Are you feeling unchallenged, stagnant, bored?
- Are you uncomfortable because you are paying too little attention to your financial situation?

Stop, look, and examine what is going on in your life. What is your dissonance trying to tell you? Your feelings of conflict, tension, fear, confusion, or discomfort are a rational survival function, as they were for Ron waiting at the elevator. Instead of ignoring them, sit back and look for the source—and then the solution.

Learn to Disengage 24

*Our life is what
our thoughts make it.*

—MARCUS AURELIUS

*No one can hurt you
without your consent.*

—ELEANOR ROOSEVELT

Have you ever been in a situation where someone or something was driving you crazy? Controlling your thoughts and emotions? Felt like the dragon was winning? We've all felt that way. So what do we do?

First, do everything you can to fix the situation. If nothing works, think about this:

121

1. You can't control other people's behavior. Never could. Never will.

2. All you can control is how you react.

Roger, an executive in a large insurance company, tells this story: "In my early years with the company, I found myself at loggerheads with a man a couple of steps up the ladder who, should he wish, could do my budding career serious harm. We were forever getting into violent confrontations. In all cases I was positive I was right, but instinctively I knew I was fighting a losing battle. One glorious day, out of the blue, I decided to never do battle with him unless it was really important. And guess what! From that day on there was never any problem that was 'really important.'"

To free yourself from the grips of a crazy-making situation, try this powerful technique:

- Visualize two interlocking gears. The first one represents your problem—the person or situation that has you in its grips. The second gear is you.

- When the problem gear twists, it forces you to twist in reaction. That problem has taken control over you. It's manipulating you.

- Now mentally and emotionally pull away—disengage––detach yourself from the problem gear. Get out of its clutches.

- From a safe distance, watch the problem gear gyrate, trying to re-engage you.

- When you disengage from your problem, you take away its power over you.

When you let people or situations get to you, you give up control of your life to them. When you disengage, you take back control. Like Roger, when he decided to fight only over "really important" things, you free yourself from the grips of the problem.

You shift from an *external* to an *internal locus* of control. In other words, you recognize that *you have the power* to control how you react. It will take time, effort, and mindfulness on your part to move into this mode, but you can do it. The more you practice, the easier it becomes. And soon you will discover this is one of the most important steps in your personal growth.

Claim *the power of you* by learning to disengage.

You Can Become More Creative

*People who say it cannot be done
Should not interrupt those who
are doing it.*

—ANONYMOUS

Creativity means more than being able to paint a picture or write a poem. It's a way of thinking, a way of living. When you come up with innovative ideas at work, when you cook interesting imaginative meals, when you play with ideas—turning them over and around in your mind examining multiple perspectives—you're being creative.

You were born with creative ability. Watch young children play. They play house and play store, have invisible friends, monsters and more. They'll create a story, a song, a new toy. And with their creativity comes enthusiasm, exuberance, and joy.

Yet, when we started school, our natural creativity tended to be squelched. We were taught to be factual, accurate, logical. Unusual, original ideas were considered "silly," and elicited frowns. Kids who repeated back exactly what they learned, with no imaginative flourishes, got better grades.

We learned *stovepipe thinking,* narrow restrictive thinking that says there is only one way to solve a problem, only one right answer. That leaves no room for creative thinking—for asking *how come, what if,* and *why not* questions. In other words, most of us were not taught effective thinking skills.

Sadly, you may know from experience that creativity-squelching can also happen in grownup work environments. Have you seen or experienced someone's new and unusual suggestion for doing something better ignored, or even ridiculed?

But all is not lost. *No matter how old you are, you can learn to think more creatively.* One of the most powerful techniques is learning to brainstorm, for that process trains your mind to be more flexible, agile and creative. Further, research has shown that when we learn to be more creative, we tend to become more vital, able, and healthy—both mentally and physically. Why? Because all parts of you are interrelated—when you change one aspect of yourself, like learning to be more creative, your whole self changes.

Brainstorming teaches us to overcome the seldom-true assumption that there is only one right answer. Doesn't it make sense to consider a wide choice of possibilities before making a decision, to give yourself the opportunity to choose the very best? For instance, when you buy a new car, wouldn't you be more likely to make a wise choice if you first investigated and looked at lots of different cars, instead of walking into a car dealer, pointing at one car and saying, "I'll take that one"?

Recently, Bill and I decide to take a mini-vacation. Instead of saying, "Let's go to the beach" and settling for that decision, we sat down with pen and paper and popped out as many ideas as we could think of—some strange, some sensible. Then we looked them all over and played with them, combining two or three ideas, changing and revamping others. We ended up having a wonderful time; we stayed home and pretended we were in a hotel, eating out every meal, exploring local sights and museums and fun shopping spots we'd never seen, and ignoring the unmade bed—pretending a maid would be in any time to do up our room. (She never showed.)

Brainstorming is a way of ensuring more elegant solutions. Almost every top corporation encourages regular brainstorming sessions. Many hire creativity trainers to teach the technique to employees.

A few years ago Deanna went to a workshop on brainstorming and was thrilled when she saw how it helped her thinking and realized the many ways she could use it. The first thing she did was introduce it to her husband Ron and their young sons. The family began brainstorming together for all sorts of decisions, like what to do about their overcrowded house. They came up with scores of ideas, like remodeling, moving to a larger home, staying put and having more money for other things, or turning the little-used formal dining room into a hobby room.

They brainstorm about where to go on vacation or what to have for dinner. Deanna and Ron found it helps them at work and personally. The boys, now eleven and fourteen, have become highly creative in many ways, and Deanna wonders if that stems from the limbering up of thought processes that brainstorming taught them.

The one absolutely necessary ingredient in creativity is *openness to new ideas*, many of which, at first, may sound ridiculous and feel threatening (see chapter 4). For instance, for millenniums Europeans believed that all heavenly bodies revolve around the earth. Then when Copernicus suggested that belief was wrong, that the earth really revolves around the sun, both the people and the church were outraged—furious. Copernicus was humiliated, ridiculed, then punished.

The point is, unless we can open up to new and weird-sounding ideas, we can make no progress, personal or scientific. Few of the scientific "truths" of the first part of the twentieth century are still considered true today; yet almost without exception, any scientist who has suggested a new (and now-accepted) way of thinking has been ridiculed.

Learning to brainstorm helps us get past our resistance to new and unfamiliar ideas. It teaches us to let our ideas flow freely and unfettered—to think without our brakes on.

How to brainstorm. Simple, fun, and effective, you can do this alone or with a group:

1. State your question. It can be about any decision you want to make. For instance, "How can I solve the problem of...?"

2. Pop out as many ideas as possible, as fast as you can. Include any and all weird ones—remember, most new ideas sound ridiculous at first. Write down every idea as it comes.

3. No criticism or comment about any of the ideas is allowed. Being critical inhibits the imagination and crushes creative thinking. The goal here is to quiet your inner critic when it sneers, "That won't work," or "What a silly

idea," or "That's already been done." The point is to *postpone judgment* in order to let ideas flow freely.

4. Generate as many ideas as possible.

5. When you've exhausted all possible ideas, sit back and look them all over. Take some time to turn them around, combine, adapt, rearrange, and play with them. Even the silly ones will contain the germ of a good idea. Have fun with this process. Laugh and play with it; humor triggers creativity.

6. Choose the best ideas to make your decision.

Brainstorming has worked so well for Bill and me that it has become a habit. We use it for work and in our personal lives––with colleagues, friends and family. Try brainstorming soon. You'll find it:

- Helps you to live, think and work more effectively.

- Helps you make better, smarter decisions.

- Is just plain fun.

R. Kirsten-Daiensai

The Power of a Smile 26

It is not the things around us which matter, but our attitude toward things.

—MARCUS AURELIUS

Did you ever notice that when you're happy, everyone around you seems happy? But when you're feeling low, everyone else seems low? It could be your facial expression, which affects not only how you feel but also how those around you feel. Moods are contagious.

We all know our moods affect our facial expressions. But did you know your facial expression also affects your mood? Smiling triggers the release of chemicals related to happiness, while frowning triggers the release of chemicals related to unhappiness. Smiling, even when you don't feel like it, makes you feel better.

After reading about this research, I decided to experiment with my own facial expressions. I found a slight smile could affect how I felt—more than I'd thought possible. But most surprising, I discovered that when I consciously assume a pleasant, somewhat smiling expression, people around me—even strangers—seem warmer, friendlier, more interested.

I was especially surprised at my experience when I went into a department store to straighten out a snafu about three wedding gifts I'd ordered. When I had bought them, I'd arranged for the store to mail them out. Within days I discovered they'd mixed up the orders and sent each gift to the wrong couple. I couldn't straighten it out on the phone so had to return to the store. Because I felt frustrated and angry, I decided it was a good time to try out my smiling theory. As I told a clerk my story, with a soft pleasant look on my face, I heard my voice sounding surprisingly gentle. I kept looking pleasant as I was shifted from one clerk to another. Getting nowhere, I (graciously) asked to speak with the manager. He treated me like royalty; the whole mess was straightened out, and I was given a sale price on everything ordered—plus an apology. What surprised me, and perhaps mattered most, was that I did not cause anyone, including myself, undue stress, for my own angry feelings seemed to dissipate once I put on a pleasant face.

Every time I gently smile the effect is positive. It's made a significant difference in my life, and I think it will in yours, too.

Have you ever watched people looking in the mirror? They smile at themselves and look so much more attractive and pleasant. Then, as they look away, they revert to their original expression. Something to think about, isn't it?

You can wear the most flattering clothes on earth, but your facial expression influences most how others perceive you. A pleasant expression is inviting; a frown turns people off. You may unconsciously frown while deep in thought or listening intently, but others may misread your feelings and react negatively. Research tells us our facial expressions can actually cause physiological changes such as in skin response and heart rate of people around us. In other words, people react physically as well as emotionally to our facial expressions.

Since we ourselves feel better when we smile or look pleasant, and others feel better and like us better that way, doesn't it make sense *to make it a habit to put on a pleasant face?*

Try this:

- Learn to relax the muscles in your forehead and around your eyes and mouth to help create a pleasant expression. A quick trick is to take a deep breath, then exhale completely; now try smiling. (Deep breathing is one of the best methods to quickly relieve tension.)

- Whether at a meeting or with any group of people— friends or strangers—when you come face-to-face with another person, even if they're deep into a frown, *smile*. You'll find almost always the other person's face will light up with a surprised and welcoming grin. Try it.

> *A smile can do wonders*
> *for your environment—*
> *inside and out.*

Be Softly Assertive 27

*Your playing small does not serve
the world. There is nothing enlightened
about shrinking so that other people
won't feel insecure around you.
We were born to manifest the glory
that is within us. And as we let our
light shine we unconsciously give
other people permission to do the same.*

—NELSON MANDELA

Sue and Russ worked together in their own business. One day Sue, while working in her office, overheard Russ chatting with Orrin, a close friend and business associate. "One of the things I like best about Sue," Russ said, "is that

I always know exactly where she stands and what she wants. It's refreshing. Living with her is easy and fun—as opposed to being around someone who won't be straightforward with you."

Russ's words were an *Aha!* for Sue, as she hadn't realized her assertiveness was as freeing for her husband as it was for herself. Since then she's found that straightforward honesty creates more harmonious relationships with everyone in her life.

I think of assertiveness as one point on a scale—about in the middle. At one extreme is passiveness—acting like a puppet and allowing others to pull your strings. At the opposite end is aggressive, demanding behavior. Either extreme is self-destructive and hurtful to those around us.

By assertiveness I mean being gently direct and honest about where you stand, what you want, and what you do not want. As Russ experienced, it liberates you and those around you. For instance, when Bill said to his long-time friend, "I worry about your smoking," Don answered, "That topic is off limits! I don't allow my children or my friends to natter at me about that!" No pouting, no anger, no arguing. Simply honest.

When you claim the freedom to be yourself, you encourage those around you to do the same. It's a win-win attitude.

Ted and Jan both had demanding jobs and two young children. An enthusiastic sort, Ted discovered and was soon captivated by golf. He started playing three nights a week with buddies, coming home after Jan had put the children to bed. Feeling put-upon, Jan didn't want to tell him he couldn't play his game, but neither was she willing to shoulder so much of the home and child care alone. Finally, one night when he got home she said, "Ted, I have no right to tell you not to play golf. But I do need time out for myself, too. Why don't we set a schedule, and I'll have three nights out for my interests, and you can still have your three nights for golf. We can have one evening a week together." Ted thought about her proposal for a while, then decided to cut down on his golf games. That was twenty-three years ago, and they're still happily married.

At least twice a month Laura flies to some far-off city to speak or attend a conference. She looks forward to using plane time to catch up on her work. On her last flight she found herself squeezed into a narrow middle seat between two men who immediately monopolized all arm rests. Laura suggested, "Why don't we share the arm rests, because I can't work without more space. Or," she said to the man on the aisle, "I could switch places with you so I'll have enough room to work." Not only did both men make arm room for Laura, they also treated her with respect and the three enjoyed a friendly flight together.

I learned a powerful lesson from Paula, a long-time friend ten years older than I, and an admired role model. At Christmastime, I invited her and her husband to a small dinner party, and she declined, saying she was coming down with a cold. Disappointed, I thoughtlessly blurted out, "Oh, Paula, you're always sick!" She answered, "You know, that really hurt my feelings when you said that." My mental reaction was that she must trust me as a friend and care about our friendship to give me that feedback.

Betsy, an attractive writer and therapist, is often asked to join professional and social groups or to serve on committees. When she is simply not interested in the proposition, instead of telling a white lie to avoid hurting people, she often answers, "I'm sorry, that doesn't work for me right now." Isn't that a fine phrase to gracefully and truthfully decline? Straightforward, honest people make life easier for themselves and for others.

To hone their professional skills, Alice and a small group of colleagues began meeting once a month. Though the individuals were bright, energetic, and successful, Alice was bothered by hearing members criticizing one another behind their backs. Finally, at a meeting she proposed that the group establish a norm: If anyone had something negative to say about another member, they would say it only to that person, in private. Her softly assertive insistence on higher standards changed the group dynamics from mediocre to trusting and productive.

If living with integrity and quality is important to you, insist upon it. When you're pressured to compromise your standards, gently refuse. When toxic people intrude on your life, softly find a way to avoid them. When people are inconsiderate of you, tell them, as Paula told me. Liberate your puppet—cut your strings and live life your way.

Try this:

- Sit back, close your eyes, and think for a moment about ways you have been effectively assertive in your life. Jot down those that worked especially well for you.

- Now, think about areas of your life where you would like to become more assertive. Write them down, along with your ideas on how to do it most effectively.

Put Your Ego in Your Pocket

28

What you are speaks so loudly I cannot hear your words.

—ANONYMOUS

As a young professor newly hired by a prestigious university, Rich was scared to death as he prepared for his first class—a big one with over two hundred students. Late into the night he wrote and rewrote his lecture, then tore it up. "But suddenly," he said, "I realized I was worrying so much about myself, about making a good impression, that I was forgetting my goal to help the students learn and be excited about this subject. I was getting tripped up by my own ego, and needed to stuff it into my back pocket. I needed to forget about myself and go out there and do the job." And he did just that, and is now one of the most popular professors at the school.

We all have egos and we all let them get in our way, sometimes. As William James wrote, "The deepest principle in human nature is the craving to be appreciated." We want to make a good impression, we want people to like us, we want to be respected. Yet when we drop our egos, when we forget about impressing, we impress the most. Whether with friends, colleagues, or loved ones, or while doing anything where you want to excel, you will invariably do better when you forget about yourself, when you focus *outward* instead of *inward*.

When we're self-conscious about how we're coming across, we don a mask, we hide the freshness and magic of our real selves. One of my favorite people is Dulcy. She's sixty-eight, a little overweight, dresses in her own unique style, and is admired and adored by all who know her. When a group of her friends tried to analyze Dulcy's magic, they decided it's because she is totally natural—no pretense, no affectation. What you see is pure authentic Dulcy. She tries to impress no one. She is competitive with no one. She is uniquely herself—a delightful character, wonderfully fun to be around. We all wished we could, like Dulcy, let go of our egos. But we agreed that is not easy.

Isn't much of the charm of Oprah and the *Today* show's Katie Couric their naturalness, their straight-forward *this is me, this is who I am* attitude?

We try so hard to be perfect, yet what is the definition of perfection? Isn't it subjective? Have you ever noticed that when good public speakers struggle for the right word, the audience becomes more involved, helping them find that word? And have you noticed that when speakers let their unique personalities show, audiences like them better? "Perfection" is boring. Unique personalities are interesting.

In my interviews with self-actualized, highly effective people, all said they consciously work on letting go of their egos. Their outward focus frees them to live lives full of meaning and purpose. *They're more concerned with feeding their souls than their egos.* And like Dulcy, they compete with no one; they seem to accept and appreciate the unique specialness of each person they meet.

As I was writing this chapter, immersed in this ego-dropping concept, my friend Emily called. I treasure her friendship, but there's always a slight sense of competition between us, which I assumed came from Emily. We had the best talk we've ever had, fresh and clear—no competitiveness, no static—and suddenly I realized that what changed was my consciously dropping my ego and concentrating on clearly hearing and communicating with Emily. "OK," I told myself, "I need to keep working on this one!" We all have egos, and some of us have to work harder to get ours out of the way.

Try this:

- With the very next person you talk to, try totally concentrating on him or her and the conversation. Let go of your ego. Forget about yourself. Then notice the tone of the interaction. Any difference?

- For the next few days, do the same with every person you talk with—at work, at home, anywhere. Be your own pure, authentic self, competing with no one. Communicate openly, clearly, sincerely. In your journal, jot down your observations.

- Do your results encourage you to make letting go of your ego a habit?

Be yourself. You are unique and special.

PART FIVE

Health Is Wealth

To Deflate Your Problems, Massage Them

29

Unrest of the spirit is a mark of life.

—KARL MENNINGER

Sometimes a problem can be so upsetting you feel consumed by it. You're so angry or upset that you can't think straight.

Once, while I was working in a professional office, a woman named Celia drove me to distraction. She interfered with my clients. She went through papers on my desk. She used my material and called it hers.

I thought of quitting, but I loved the work. Finally, about to blow, I came home, sat at my desk, and wrote and wrote and wrote, pouring out everything that had happened and how I felt, turning the situation over and around and inside-out, trying to see all aspects. After about forty-five minutes I found myself writing, "What matters most is not what Celia is doing, but how I handle it. That will define the kind of person I am. Five years from now, how I reacted will be what matters most."

The most amazing thing happened after that. Nothing Celia did bothered me. Her actions floated past me with no effect. And the interesting thing is, very soon she stopped her offensive behavior and started treating me with respect. That was fifteen years ago, and sure enough, my memories of that experience are only positive. Celia's behavior did not define me, it defined Celia. Only my behavior can define me. And I am sure that, while feeling so stressed by Celia's actions, I could not have achieved that awareness without massaging the problem.

Here are two ways to massage a problem:

1. Sit down with a fat notebook or at the word processor. Write out all your frustrations and feelings, worries and questions about the issue—whatever comes out—until

you find yourself slowing down. Turn the problem over and around in your mind, play with it. Write about it from as many different perspectives as you can—yours, the other person's, an objective bystander's, a visiting Martian's, five years into the future, and any other viewpoints you can think of. Keep on writing and after a while *your answer will emerge*.

2. Or you can verbally massage the problem with someone whose judgment you trust and respect. Talk about it, massage it the same way you'd write, looking at every angle, playing with ideas and solutions.

It's amazing how well massaging your problems works. It's as if you had the answer in your subconscious all along and just had to let it out. Not only does this method help you find the answers you seek, but you'll find the actual process of massaging and processing a problem is deeply satisfying.

Meditation Works 30

Life is what we make it;
always has been,
always will be.

—GRANDMA MOSES

Because one of my goals as a first-year graduate student was to learn how our minds and bodies interact, I went to the Menninger Foundation to study under pioneering biofeedback researchers Elmer and Alyce Green. I learned a stunning lesson: As we meditated, we watched scientific instruments register our brain waves slowing to a state of deep relaxation, our muscles relaxing, and our heart rates slowing.

Twenty-five hundred years ago the Buddha taught that our minds are like a tree full of chattering monkeys, and this endless chattering keeps us from seeing our real selves. He said we need to quiet our minds, and the best way is through meditation. Since then, billions of people have benefited from that advice. Our noisy mind chatter jumps from thought to thought, and gets louder and louder as the normal stresses of life build up during the day. But then, when you sit quietly for a few moments, meditating, your stress level slides back down to normal. You feel rebalanced, more at peace, more centered. Meditation helps you to live and love and work more effectively.

One of the most surprising benefits of regular meditation is that your mind gets sharper and your concentration better. You'll find solutions to problems and creative ideas suddenly come to you. For instance, often when I've been struggling to explain a complex thought, the right words spontaneously emerge as I meditate. Albert Einstein and scores of other scientists have said their most brilliant ideas came to them while they were in a state of deep relaxation, their minds quiet.

Listen on the inside. Inside your head, in a quiet place, sitting, waiting, is the answer.

The physical, mental, and emotional benefits of meditation are well-documented. Stress affects every part of you and relieving it makes you more healthy. Stress renders your immune system less effective; for instance, it makes you five times more likely to get a cold. And you certainly enjoy life more when feeling mellow and centered. So doesn't it make sense to take some simple steps to become healthier, happier, and more fully-functioning?

Here are the basic steps in meditation:

1. The goal is to quiet your mind, and to do that you block out the chatter by concentrating on one simple word or phrase.

2. Sit comfortably in a chair, shoulders relaxed, feet on the floor, hands in your lap, eyes closed. Or if you need to rest your back, you can lie down on your back, knees propped up a bit (but don't fall asleep).

3. Begin by taking a few deep breaths, exhaling completely. Then, breathing naturally, repeat in your mind each time you exhale a word such as *one, love, peace, relax,* or *calm.* Choose a word that feels peaceful for you. If you prefer, repeat a phrase from a favorite prayer.

4. When extraneous thoughts come into your mind, and they will, let them pass on through. It will take you a while to completely quiet your mind. Don't worry about it.

5. Continue meditating for twenty minutes. You'll feel your mind and body relax into that peaceful state somewhere between sleeping and waking. When you're extra busy, even a few minutes of meditating is better than none.

6. When you're through, give yourself a minute or two before getting up.

7. Practice meditating once each day. In between times, try mini-medits. For instance, sitting at your desk or before a meeting, quietly close your eyes, take a few deep breaths, and meditate for a few minutes.

8. The more you practice, the more quickly your mind will quiet and the more effective meditating becomes for you.

How about sitting back now, closing your eyes, and quieting your mind?

Exercise for Your Body
—and Your Brain

31

You are in the process of change.
You might as well become
what you want.

—ANONYMOUS

Mike, a forty-three-year-old patent attorney, works under "impossible pressure" for a major software firm. "The one thing," he says, "that keeps me mentally sharp and balanced is working out at the club every morning. If I miss a session I can tell the difference all day. I can't think as clearly, I can't handle the stress, I make poor decisions."

Mike's experience supports research that shows regular exercise contributes to our *physical, mental, and emotional* well-being.

161

A growing body of evidence tells us:

- Exercise is a basic human need and the closest thing to the fountain of youth. Our bodies are meant to be used.

- Regular vigorous exercise alleviates or prevents mental and physical deterioration. Most of the weakness and frailty we blame on aging is due not to getting older but to inactivity.

- The brains of people who exercise work better—especially memory, mental flexibility, response time, and creativity. One recent study found physically active people are less likely to get Alzheimer's disease.

- Exercise is one of the most powerful factors in stress management—it releases your stress.

- Exercise reduces the risk of depression and anxiety.

- Regular exercise boosts self-esteem. You'll feel more alive, vital, and energetic—physically and emotionally.

- Vigorous exercise helps you keep your weight down by using calories and because fit muscles utilize more calories.

- Exercise reduces bone loss, reducing the risk of osteoporosis in both men and women.
- Exercise is now viewed as an important preventative factor in scores of diseases including diabetes, some diseases of the eye, obesity, cardiovascular disease, some cancers, depression, and osteoarthritis. In other words, a healthy mind and body resist disease.
- People who exercise enjoy better sex.
- People who exercise look better!

This all sounds a bit like snake-oil salesman stuff, doesn't it? But it's so wonderfully true. Think of the power you have to improve your life—in so many ways—by deciding to exercise.

If you're not exercising now, you may have to push yourself a bit to get started, to overcome inertia. The more we sit around, the less we feel like getting up and moving. (And please, first check with your doctor.)

Once you start exercising regularly, you'll enjoy it so much that it could become a favorite part of your day. While you work out and afterwards you'll feel a natural high from the endorphins produced by your brain. That's nature—bribing you.

How to make exercise work for you:

1. Start out with a half-hour workout three times a week. Then, if time allows, work up to forty-five minutes a day, five to seven days a week. The rewards will be obvious to you—and to those around you.

2. Brisk walking is great. Other ways include workout tapes, a stationary or regular bike, a treadmill—anything that gets you moving.

3. Include weight training in your exercise routine; it is "the only type of exercise that can substantially slow, and even reverse, the declines in muscle mass, bone density, and strength that were once considered inevitable consequences of aging," reported the *Harvard Health Letter*. Use simple weights at home with the help of written guidelines (see the reading suggestions at the end of the book) or join a health club. Working with

weights helps you make sure all your muscles are fit. I had back problems all my adult life and was told by an orthopedic surgeon nothing could be done; but soon after joining a health club eight years ago the problem disappeared. It seems weak muscles allowed my spine to be pulled out of alignment.

4. Don't limit exercising to your regular workouts. Find creative ways to be more active throughout your day. Instead of taking the elevator, walk up steps. Instead of jockeying for a close-in parking space, park farther away and walk. Use that wonderful body of yours!

5. Try combining your workouts with getting together with friends. Instead of meeting people for lunch or for a drink after work, meet for an hour's walk. You'll be amazed at how much better conversation can be while walking together in the fresh air. And there's a social benefit to joining a fitness club. We've met some of our most active, alive and interesting friends there, for growing people are out exercising. Dave, the dynamic executive, met his wife while working out at his club.

6. Make exercise a priority in your life, like brushing your teeth and eating. When my children were young and I was running a business and trying to be a great wife and mother, I used to feel selfish whenever I took time out to exercise. But finally it dawned on me that I needed to be fit to function well in all those roles. I decided it was my responsibility to make exercise a priority, and it's remained so because whenever I skip it, everything goes downhill.

   Start exercising today—and have fun with it! Enjoy feeling and looking your very best.

Nothing Tastes as Good as Being Slim Feels

32

*If you always do what you
    always did,
You'll always get what
    you always got*

.—ANONYMOUS

*Feeling in control is an internal
trait that can be learned, just like
its opposite—helplessness.*

—RICHARD RESTAK, NEUROLOGIST

My role model for getting and staying slim is Helen. All her adult life she was overweight, and every year she found herself gaining a few more pounds. Finally, one warm spring day she tried on a favorite dress—and it was too small. "I don't need to let this happen," she thought. At that moment, she decided to take action.

You, too, have probably experienced that mental clicking over, the *Aha!* that switches you onto a new path. Helen's *Aha!* was, "I'm getting fat because I eat too much. All I need to do is eat less." She decided to keep eating all her favorite foods but to cut all portions by a third. And she discovered she didn't miss the extra food (well, hardly ever). Though she felt little hunger, her weight gradually dropped to a healthy level and has remained there ever since. She feels better, looks better, is happier—and her clothes look great on her.

Our body weight strongly affects how we feel about ourselves, our self-concept, our sense of competence, our very identity. And the good news is, we *can* control our weight. Yes, it's more of a challenge for some of us: Our genes can make it more difficult, the eating habits we learned as children can sabotage us, and self-control is easier for some than for others. Don't hesitate to enlist support from groups such as Weight Watchers or Overeaters Anonymous. Do whatever works best for you.

None of us is alone in our weight-control struggle. It is a national problem—one in three adults is obese, and statistics tell us Americans are growing fatter every year. And this increase is *not* the result of our genes; they have not changed. We are simply eating too much!

Obesity is our second leading *preventable* cause of death after smoking. That word—preventable—means we won't get fat unless we eat more calories than we burn, and that boils down to will power. As Winston Churchill said, "All great things are decided…by willpower. Whoever has it will finally prevail."

Yet we all know changing our eating habits is not easy. But you *can* do it—and forevermore be thankful. The good news is that exercising your will power is like exercising your muscles—the more you do it, the easier it gets, and then it becomes a habit. "Each time we exercise will power," wrote geneticist Dean Hamer, "we rewire our brain…which makes it easier the next time."

Because overweight people have significantly more health problems as years go by, changing your eating habits can not only enhance your enjoyment of life, it *extends* your time to enjoy.

This doesn't mean following some unrealistic ideal of thinness; you'll just torture yourself. You can't look like you did when you were twenty-one, but you *can* look terrific for your present age.

Yet for some of you losing weight is simply not worth the struggle. Dulcy, my delightful friend adored by many, is overweight and has *never* gone on a diet. She loves to cook and to eat and chooses to remain the way she is—so *that* is the right choice for her. And it may be for you, too. *You* know when you weigh too much. How others respond to you, how you feel, how you function, and your mirror tell you when and if it's time to make some changes.

> *Nature is always hinting at us,*
> *It hints over and over again,*
> *And suddenly we take the hint.*

—ROBERT FROST

Here are twelve steps for lifelong weight control:

1. The most important factor in weight control is *knowledge*. We've all heard heavy people complaining that a slim friend eats more than they do and never gains weight. It is as much *what* you eat as *how much*. *Calories do count.* Fat, at 9 calories per gram, has more than twice as many calories as protein or carbohydrates, both at 4 calories per gram. And those few extra calories add up fast; for instance, you would gain 10 pounds per year if you ate just one extra butter patty (100 calories) per day.

2. Crash and fad diets simply do not work. Yes, you may lose weight—for a while. But since you're not changing your eating habits, you'll regain it as soon as you go off the diet. *The only way to keep your weight under control is to learn—and consistently practice—good eating habits.*

3. To discover where your extra calories come from (especially hidden fat), for several weeks *keep a journal* of everything you eat. In my graduate school nutrition classes we were asked to do that. At first I bristled at the assignment, considering it busy work. But what a

revelation! I'd thought I ate a healthy low-fat diet, and was shocked at my fat consumption—from things like popcorn, peanuts, salad dressings, unskinned chicken, even "just a dab" of sour cream on my baked potato. I learned that many of my calories were hidden or ignored (a bit of self-delusion). I learned I needed to be honest with myself. I learned *we lie loudest when we lie to ourselves.*

4. Learn to *read labels* for fat content. Buy a little reference booklet giving you the nutritional content of food.

5. *Exercise* every day (see chapter 31). To prevent weight gain, you need to expend as many calories as you take in. Not only do fit muscles metabolize more calories, exercise also tends to stabilize your appetite.

6. *Learn to eat slim in restaurants.* Order broiled instead of fried, red sauces instead of cream sauces, salad dressings on the side, no butter on bread (well, maybe just a tiny dab now and then), and no sour cream on baked potatoes (you'll be surprised how delicious plain potatoes

and bread taste). As you change to eating less fat, you'll find your tastes changing, with high-fat foods starting to taste greasy and heavy to you.

7. *Eat plants!* Government nutrition guidelines tell us we need only 3 to 4 ounces of meat or other protein food per day; any extra is converted to energy or, if unused, to fat. Instead, eat lots of fruits and vegetables. Try seasoning with a little meat, as many Asians do, instead of making it the centerpiece of your meal. Nature photographers Keith and Antje noticed their friends who ate more vegetables seemed to have more energy and were sick less, so decided to change their diet. Within weeks they felt better, and Keith's cholesterol dramatically dropped. (Medical experts from around the world, sponsored by the American Institute for Cancer Research, met and reported that eating a plant-based diet— with less meat and more fruits, vegetables, legumes, and grains—together with exercising and controlling weight, can prevent 30 to 40% of cancers.)

8. You'll feel more satisfied longer after eating *high fiber foods*, such as fresh fruits and whole grains. They're better for you, too.

9. *Listen to your body!* Stop eating and push back from the table as soon as you feel satisfied. In other words, stop before you feel *full*—the signal that you've eaten too much.

10. *Drink at least eight glasses of water a day*, especially before meals. It's good for you, and it fills you up.

11. *Avoid temptation* by keeping only healthy, low-fat snacks in the house. At the beginning of the week prepare a batch of raw vegetables for snacking. Eat pretzels instead of potato chips, nonfat whole grain crackers instead of high-fat crackers, half an apple instead of a cookie, bread with jam instead of butter (jam has less than half the calories of butter). And if you love ice cream or frozen yogurt, eat *just a tiny dish* of the low-fat or nonfat varieties; they're surprisingly good. To satisfy our chocolate urge, Bill and I sometimes eat four or five M&Ms in the evening—17 calories worth.

12. *Create a pleasant place to eat.* Serve your food attractively, eat slowly, savor every bite. Consider not watching TV or reading as you eat, for then you don't notice when you're eating too much.

Use the Power of Your Mind: All of the above won't help a bit if your mind hasn't clicked over to a new way of thinking about eating. Here are some mental techniques that work for others:

- Lovely Rondi, a fifty-year-old real estate leader, says her staying-slim trick is visualizing herself on her next vacation—looking great. Right now in her mind's eye she's looking svelte on a beach in Hawaii. "My biggest challenge," she says, "is the goodies my husband brings home from the store. I keep things like oranges and nonfat cottage cheese in the house to help me resist."

- My husband Bill visualizes himself walking downtown and glimpsing himself in a store window looking slim and fit.

- Karen, who four years after her divorce has decided she's ready to start dating, reminds herself, whenever tempted to overeat, how consistently she's had feedback that most men *really prefer* slim women.

- Whenever I'm tempted to eat some succulent goodie, like an innocent little chocolate bar, on my mental scale I weigh the alternatives, asking, "Is this worth getting fat for?" or "Am I willing to walk an extra 59.23 minutes to burn off these 308 calories?" or "Will I be sorry an hour from now?"

- When Greg, who is trying to take off a few extra pounds that have crept up on him, feels hunger pangs, he remembers, "I *can't* lose weight without feeling hunger, because that's the signal that my body is using its extra fat."

- And remember Helen, who tells herself, "I don't need that much food," and just eats less.

- Try any or all of these mental techniques or think of a new one that works for you.

  You *can* do it, and you'll love the results!

PART SIX

The Process of Growing

Visualize Your
Future Self

33

*The best way to predict
your future is to create it.*

—STEPHEN COVEY

Most Olympic medal winners and world-class athletes will tell you visualization plays a key role in their success. Every day before competing they sit quietly and see, feel, and experience themselves executing each part of their performance—perfectly. Later, when they actually compete, they automatically slip into their visualized behavior. Jack Nicklaus said his golf shot is 10% swing, 40% setup and stance, and 50% mental picture.

Peak performers use visualization because it works—in sports, personal life, and business. Researchers found that the most successful business people mentally practice what they want to say and do before important meetings. Other effective people do the same. The evening before a scheduled surgery, cardiologist Robert visualizes step-by-step the planned surgical procedure—first a perfect operation, then what he would do if he encountered certain problems.

When you visualize the way you want to do something or the kind of person you want to be, your mind, feelings, and muscles actually practice that experience. For instance, when athletes visualize themselves performing perfectly, actual physical responses in the involved muscles can be detected by instruments.

As one of the majority of Americans whose greatest fear is public speaking, the first time I was asked to speak to a group of professionals about my research on how adults grow, I cringed. The idea of trying to sound coherent in front of an auditorium full of people was terrifying. But I really wanted to share my research, and I also knew the only way to break through my numbing fear was to go ahead and do it. What got me through was lots of practice, along with visualizing every detail of my talk—posture, delivery, humor, letting go of my ego (see chapter 28), even the

180

audience's enthusiastic response. Then, immediately before going on, I found a secluded room, sat quietly, and visualized again. It worked. The audience was enthusiastic and I actually enjoyed the whole experience. Their questions went on so long the moderator had to interrupt to continue the program. And now, a few years and many talks later, I've shifted from cowering in the corner to loving it, even becoming a bit of a ham.

The point is, visualization works. If you want to become a better ice skater or public speaker or a more vigorous, growing, interesting, fully functioning person, you can make that happen. Seeing your goal in your mind's eye helps it become a reality.

To begin:

1. Sit down and think about ways you want to change. You might want to enhance how you relate to others, how you react to stress, your humor and playfulness, your intellectual, moral and spiritual self, your mental and physical health and vitality, your work and achievements and contributions to society—whatever is important to you. *Write it all down. You are the program-*

mer; write your program. As new ideas come to you, add them to your list.

2. Find a quiet place, sit down, close your eyes, breathe deeply, and relax (relaxation frees your brain to create images). Now, select one thing you want to change.

3. Then, in your mind picture yourself being the way you want to be. For instance, if you want to laugh more, see yourself howling with laughter at a TV show or with friends, or using gentle humor to ease a stressful situation. Include in your visualization how you would feel, how you would sound, how you would look. Build on your image. Expand it. Relish it. Make it a reality. If you can see it, you can achieve it.

4. Finally, when you're satisfied with your progress on one goal, move on to the next.

You'll be surprised at how well visualization can work for you. And how good it feels. But remember, we change not in giant leaps, but one small step at a time. You have the rest of your life, so be patient with yourself. Relax and relish the process of becoming the person you want to be.

Growing Means Risking

34

*Behold the turtle.
He makes progress only
when he sticks his neck out.*

—ANONYMOUS

Paul, my husband Bill's father, stayed in the same job throughout his working life, though it was never what he *really* wanted to do. After retiring Paul confessed to Bill—who'd tried two professions before finding the one he loved—that in hindsight he wished he'd taken more risks. Too many of us, when we reach a crossroads choose the secure path, the way of least resistance. We then spend the rest of our lives regretting that decision. Robert Frost said it well:

> *Two roads diverged in a wood, and I—*
> *I took the one less traveled by,*
> *and that has made all the difference.*

Every time you go forward, you venture into the unknown. Every time you try out new ways of thinking and doing, you risk leaving your comfortable, familiar, safe world—and that takes courage! It's like the lobster that must shed its shell to grow; he is more vulnerable until he grows a new shell. It's like a baby learning to walk; every step she takes challenges her balance, and she falls and hurts a little. But how else can one learn to walk?

While you are in transition you feel more vulnerable, and you may take a tumble or two, and you may hurt. Yet how else can you grow? As Aurobindo wrote, "Life is one of

continually falling on your face, getting up, brushing yourself off, looking sheepishly at God, and taking another step."

Some thoughts to ponder:

- Unless you accept a challenge, you can never feel the
  exhilaration of victory.

- After taking a few small risks and experiencing some
  successes and some stumbles, you'll discover that stum-
  bling doesn't hurt that much and success feels
  wonderful, so you'll become more confident—even excited—about risking again.

- Remember, growing means risking; the alternative leads
  to stagnation.

With each developmental step, like trying any of the
suggestions in this book, you stick your neck out and progress
into new territory. This is the only way you can grow.

For instance, women and men who return to school at
mid-life risk having friends and family feel threatened or
resentful. They risk facing fellow students who are younger

and more familiar with current thinking. They risk their hard-won financial security.

Yet, once you commit yourself to a new path, the most amazing things begin to happen. New doors open to you. Unexpected opportunities you never dreamed of come your way. You get onto a track that was there waiting for you and meet others on that track, and you help each other along the way. You discover momentum, energy, exhilaration you've never known.

At forty-seven, Joyce was feeling more and more confined and unfulfilled in the laboratory where she did research in molecular biology. She realized that to many she had a dream job, but something felt wrong. All her life she had loved to draw, but she'd never pursued that passion, mostly because of pressure from family and teachers to go into science where, after all, she did excel.

Then one day, on impulse, she visited a nearby art school. That was all she needed. Her savings allowed her to take a leave of absence from her job and enroll in the school. For four years she loved every minute of learning and experimenting with new art forms and techniques. Now she's building her career as a commercial artist, presently illustrating a children's book. She seems to have blossomed in every way. Whereas before she'd been serious and studious, now she laughs and jokes, revealing a sense of humor no one knew was there. She's met a group of supportive close friends she feels more attuned to than any she's ever known. Joyce found the path that is right for her.

Jot down your responses to these questions:

1. Have I avoided trying a new path because of the risk involved?

2. What is the worst thing that could happen if I take that risk and fail?

3. What is the best thing that could happen if I take that risk and succeed?

4. If I take that risk, what will most likely happen?

5. Five years from now, how will I probably feel if I did not take that risk?

Dare to find the path of your heart—and follow it. You'll discover new energy and enthusiasm—even exhilaration—as you pursue your heartfelt goal.

> *Whatever you can do,*
> *or dream you can, begin it.*
> *Boldness has genius, power*
> *and magic in it.*
> *BEGIN IT NOW.*
>
> —GOETHE

Grow Your Brain 35

*What we nurture in
ourselves will grow;
that is nature's eternal law.*

—GOETHE

Can mental challenge stimulate your brain to grow? We
now know the answer is a resounding *yes!* Use it or lose it
works for our brains, too.

Caged rats, researchers discovered, that are exposed to
mental challenges such as ever-changing toys like wheels,
ladders, and mazes grow bigger and better brains than those
given food and water, but nothing to stimulate their brains.
And—most interesting of all—*age makes no difference!* Brains
of old rats, when challenged, grow as much as those of the

very young. And there's more. Challenged old rats stay younger, healthier, more vigorous. They learn better, have better memories, and are better problem solvers (like learning to negotiate difficult mazes). And they have more fun—they romp and play right along with the youngsters.

The good news is, the same is true in humans: As long as we live (if we have no serious brain disease), when our brains are challenged, they grow. The idea that older brains inevitably deteriorate is simply *not true*. At any age, unused brains atrophy and stimulated brains remain healthy—and grow!

"It is possible for an eighty-year-old to have the brain of a thirty-year-old. The secret is simply use," said neurologist Arnold Scheibel, M.D. Your brain, like your body, needs regular workouts. People who exercise their minds seldom go downhill mentally.

For example, Georgia O'Keeffe continued to create some of her greatest art almost until her death at age ninety-nine. And there's George Burns, who remained mentally active and delightfully funny until he died, also at ninety-nine. Even from centuries past, when most folks never reached fifty, we see people like Sir Isaac Newton, mathematician and physicist, who continued to produce brilliant original ideas until his death—at eighty-five.

And the good news is people who exercise their brains tend to remain more healthy in every way—physically, mentally, emotionally. Your mind and your body are an integrated system; changing one part, like your brain, affects all the rest of you.

Here's how to keep your brain healthy and growing:

- Get involved in a wide variety of activities. Every one of your senses needs stimulation. Through MRI brain scans we've learned that specific areas of our brains grow relative to which sense is challenged.

- Pursue your present interests but develop new ones, too. Here's your excuse to take up painting or line dancing, the pan flute or Eastern philosophies. Learn a new skill, study a new subject. Build things with your hands, get involved in the community. Find things you like to do.

- Keep your mental antennae rotating, looking for new experiences, new challenges, new things to learn.
- Ask questions, search for answers. Keep your curiosity alive and active.

If this all sounds like a big job, don't worry. Your brain doesn't have to have *continual* stimulation. Our normal way of learning is to surge ahead, then fall back and rest, as a wave surging onto the beach then needs time to fall back. Take time to integrate, to ponder, to savor. Then go for it! And have fun with it!

Learning Is Growing, Growing Is Learning

36

Happiness comes only when
we push our brains and
hearts to the farthest reaches
of which we are capable.

—LEO ROSTEN

The greatest genius will not be worth
much if he pretends to draw exclusively
on his own resources.

—GOETHE

There is no knowledge
that is not power.

—RALPH WALDO EMERSON

Let's pretend. I'll hand you one small piece of a giant jigsaw puzzle. Hold it in your hand. Study it. What do you see? Let this one small image represent your present view of the world. Let the completed puzzle represent the wisdom of the world. It will take you more than a lifetime to put the whole puzzle together, but with each piece you add, the wiser you become.

Some people are satisfied with a few small pieces, with one clearly defined view of reality. And to them, adding new pieces—new dimensions—feels threatening, confusing and uncomfortable.

Do you know people who have stopped learning? Are they interesting to be around? Are they opinionated, narrow, lonely, unhappy? Have they grown since you've known them?

On the other hand, do you know people who are ever-curious, who like kittens explore every nook and cranny of life that catches their interest? Who keep their minds open and searching for new information to help them fill out their picture of life? Are they dynamic, vital, growing, happy? Do they seem old? Do others search out their company?

Life is meant to be a never-ending education. Dr. K. Warner Schai, famed expert on mental development in adults, found that middle-aged people who avoid mental stimulation decline faster—mentally and physically—as they grow older. In contrast, ever-learning people tend to experience almost no mental and far less physical decline.

Just as Chinese women of yore cringed in pain from feet bound to restrict normal growth, restricting our inborn imperative to learn and grow as long as we live constricts and contorts spirit and soul.

When we stop learning, mummifying ourselves within our old familiar ideas and ways of thinking, we wither. We fossilize. We will never "know it all," and when we think we do, we stop learning and become old. It's as simple as that. And think about this for a moment: *We cannot grow without learning—nor can we learn without growing.* When we learn we expand our understanding of life—and *that* is growing!

This is one of the reasons ninety-two-year-old Helen attracts people of all ages. She's curious. She reads. She asks penetrating questions. She welcomes differing opinions. Her mental antennae continually rotate—searching for a broader picture. A few years ago she fell and broke her foot, and the doctor came in to see her and said, "I saw your age on the chart and expected to meet an old lady. In no way are you an old lady." He's right!

I need to make this important point for you: There is a difference between basic everyday learning and transformative learning. Basic learning refers to learning something new to you, like a new word. It doesn't change you, but it fills you out. And we need that!

Transformative learning unsettles. It challenges your habitual way of thinking. It forces you to restructure your mind into new, more mature ways of understanding—and *to grow* we need that.

For instance, my view of life was transformed when I visited China in 1985. The focus of our trip was to learn about present-day life in China, and for months in advance

I read book after book about it. While there, we had prear-ranged meetings with many small groups of men and women from various professions and walks of life. Slowly, maybe unintentionally, the horror of the ravages of the Cultural Revolution emerged. Honored professors and brilliant mu-sicians were beaten, tortured, and killed by ferocious fanatics. Millions of books—treasured ancient texts, modern medi-cal tomes, philosophical masterpieces—were burned. Thousands of years of scholarly and artistic treasures were destroyed.

Nothing impeded the marauders, for the government instigated the carnage. Yet no protestors, no editorials, no citizen groups spoke out, for all feared punishment or death.

Before that experience I had always felt impatient with protestors, particularly unruly noisy ones whose views dif-fered from mine. For someone raised in a prim, well-behaved Midwest community, they seemed out of line. But in China I glimpsed a bigger picture; I realized that it is those very protestors—*even those most radical*—who keep our society in balance. That only when the voices of dissent are silenced can monstrosities such as the Cultural Revolution and the Holocaust emerge, and take over.

Some ways to ensure lifelong learning:

- *Be open* (we've said this before but it's so critical for growth it bears repeating). We simply *cannot learn* unless we welcome new ideas, even—and especially—when they feel uncomfortable, for they challenge our habitual way of viewing the world. All changes, even positive ones, are scary.

- *Read. Read. Read.* Search out new topics to learn and be excited about. Make it your goal to understand different viewpoints. For instance, read authors from different races, cultures, and religions to learn their perspectives.

- *Get to know people different from you.* Try to understand their way of thinking. Explore all facets of life's prism. It's too easy to interpret the world only from our own narrow angle.

- *Volunteer* to teach or help people from other walks of life, and learn from them, too.

- *Take classes* in anything you think might interest you at your local community college or wherever you can find sources of new learning.

- Never be afraid to *ask questions* when you don't understand. You won't look stupid. Stupid is not finding out as much as you can. When I returned to graduate school at mid-life, most of my classmates were decades younger. I had been out of school so long and was so far behind on the subjects I was petrified of asking a question—sure I would sound foolish. But finally my curiosity took over, and every time I asked a question classmates would comment, "Yeah, I wondered about that, too."

- Watch *valuable TV specials* on topics new to you.

- Learn to *use the Internet*. It's new and exciting and you really don't want to miss out on the almost infinite learning that could be at your fingertips, do you? And just learning to do it will grow your brain!

- As much as your time and budget allow, *travel to learn*. In 1984 Russ and Sue traveled to Russia to compare the attitudes of people living under Communism with those of Americans living in a democracy. Many of their former ideas of life and people drastically changed as a result of that trip. For instance, they found that constant repression seemed to have seriously stifled creative thinking in men, women—even children.

- *Listen mindfully to others!* You can learn from everyone.
- In other words, *be forever curious*—never stop exploring, asking questions, and finding ways to investigate, learn, and grow.

The world is changing faster than we can conceive. New technologies, countries changing names and borders faster than we can buy new maps, and scientific breakthroughs continually shuffle our view of life and nature. It's all there, inviting you to get on board. Come on along!

Pacing Helps You Grow

37

To be what we are, and to become what we are capable of becoming, is the only end of life.

—ROBERT LOUIS STEVENSON

Want another hot tip? One of the best ways to be sure you and your brain keep right on growing is to expose yourself to *pacing*. What is *pacing*? It's like playing tennis with a slightly better player; your game tends to improve. It's like reading a book that at first seems like gibberish, but you keep working until you understand this new way of thinking, and you expand your mind. The better tennis player or the challenging book can pace you to *stretch* beyond your present level.

Just as at dog races, where mechanical rabbits zoom in front of racing greyhounds to pace them toward greater speed, challenging ideas pace us toward personal growth. At the beginning of my graduate work, I read a book by a leader in my field and thought, "He's a terrible writer; this is nonsense." But since I *had* to learn about these concepts, I kept struggling with it. When finally I figured it out, I realized his writing had seemed nonsensical because his thinking had been beyond me. I learned that only by stretching and straining to understand could I move to a new level of thinking.

Your pacer—be it tennis player or book or mechanical rabbit—can't be *too far* beyond you, or you'll give up in frustration. For optimal pacing your challenge must be *just one step beyond* your present level. *You grow not in giant leaps, but one step at a time.*

The significant effect of pacing was one of the most stunning findings in my research on how and why some adults continue to grow and mature, while others do not. Participants in the study who reported being paced *to the point of feeling discomfort*, as they struggled to understand more complex thinking, grew the most. Their minds surged to new horizons. Like playing tennis with a better player, when you stretch and strain, maybe even hurt a little, your game improves.

Dave, a top executive in a large West Coast corporation, says a good place to find pacing is at work. "Instead of avoiding people who challenge you, seek out interaction with those willing to give you suggestions and constructive criticism. It's an opportunity waiting for you."

When you think about it, doesn't pacing as a stimulus for growth make sense?

Try this:

1. Be on the lookout for pacing opportunities—people or experiences that can help you stretch to new levels of behavior, ability, understanding, and thinking.

2. When you feel a little discomfort as you stretch, keep at it because that means it's working.

3. Develop vital alive relationships with a wide variety of stimulating people. Include many who are different from you in background, interests, thinking. How will you find alive relationships? When you are out there doing interesting things, open and curious, learning and growing, they will find you.

4. In areas where you choose to improve or grow, push yourself to excel. It's exhilarating—and it works.

I would rather be ashes than dust.
I would rather my spark should burn out in a
brilliant blaze
Than it should be stifled in dry-rot.
I would rather be a superb meteor,
Every atom of me in magnificent glow,
Than a sleepy and permanent planet.
Man's chief purpose is to live, not exist.
I shall not waste my days trying
to prolong them.
I shall use my time.

—JACK LONDON

PART SEVEN

The Power of Communicating Well

The Power
of Listening

38

*Wise men talk because they
have something to say;
fools talk because they
have to say something.*

—PLATO

No charm equals that of a good listener. Eleanor Roosevelt endeared many with her rare skill for giving her full, undivided attention to the person she was with. She made everyone she talked with feel valuable and important.

I thought I was a good listener until I listened to the tape recording of a telephone meeting with Anna, my graduate school advisor. I was shocked to hear myself constantly interrupting her. Even though each interruption was an enthusiastic comment on her ideas, it still broke her train of thought. Since then I've been trying to be mindful of not interrupting when another is speaking, except for the occasional *uh-huh* affirming that I'm hearing what's being said.

Recently while my husband and I were out to dinner, he commented on a woman a few tables away. "That woman is fascinating to watch. She's listening so intently to what her partner is saying. Her eyes are on him, she's leaning forward, giving verbal feedback—not enough to interrupt but letting him know she's hearing, and she's also holding up her end of the conversation. She's the kind of woman I wouldn't notice on the street, but she looks attractive now because she's so interested." We wondered if good listening is so rare that such an example stands out.

If you want to become a better communicator, listen to yourself. Are you *really* listening? Are you letting the other person finish without interrupting? Are you talking more than you're listening? While you're talking do your listeners start to fidget? Do their eyes wander, glaze over? While someone is talking are you impatiently thinking about what you're going to say next? Real listening embodies careful attention, patience, and truly *wanting* to understand what the other person is saying.

Try the following experiment:

1. For the next week, whenever you talk with your mate, family, friends, or colleagues, listen to what they say with your *full, undivided attention.*

2. Try to get into *their* perspective instead of hearing through yours.

3. Don't dilute your attention by thinking about what you'll say next.

4. Let them totally finish what they're trying to tell you before you speak.

5. Respond briefly and thoughtfully, making it clear, maybe by feeding back to them your understanding of what they said, that you heard and understood.

6. After a week of good listening, notice if and how your relationships have changed.

We've all known people who talk too much. It's difficult to be around them. As Voltaire said, "The secret of being a bore is to tell everything." And aside from being boring, being *talked at* is insulting. As I keep reminding myself, we learn nothing when we're talking; we learn only when we listen.

And being listened to—attentively—feels good. It's flattering. It fosters good relationships.

Listen to Understand:
The Power of Empathy *39*

If there is any secret of success,
it lies in the ability to get to
the other person's point of view
and see things from his angle
as well as your own.

—HENRY FORD

As I struggled to clearly explain empathy for you, the reader, I talked it over with my friend Lisa, a thirty-seven-year-old meteorologist. She had been looking for a more challenging job and had finally received responses from three application letters—all negative. As we talked, suddenly Lisa's face lit up. "You know, I wrote those letters telling them what I want in a job. I didn't really think about it from *their* point of view or in terms of *their* needs. I didn't

213

empathize with them at all, did I?" She then wrote another application letter, this time imagining herself in the shoes of the recipient, telling how she could help that organization achieve its goals. She got the job.

It's easy to confuse sympathy with empathy. Sympathy means feeling sorry for another. Empathy means feeling *with* another. "You poor thing," and "I feel so sorry for you," reflect sympathy. "Sounds as if you really feel hurt," and "I get the feeling you're totally frustrated" reflect empathy. It's putting yourself into the shoes of another, mentally and emotionally sharing that person's experience.

To become more empathic:

1. *Listen to understand* another's experience *from his or her point of view.* Try to see the world through that person's eyes.

2. Try to unconditionally accept that person—without judgment or criticism—as a valued and unique individual.

3. Let the other person *know* you understand—with attentive listening, body language, and words.

Empathic teachers, psychotherapists, and parents are more effective because of their ability to understand. And empathy is absolutely essential for a deeply satisfying, empowering marriage—for a union where soul meets soul.

> *Empathy means listening with your heart as well as your head.*

Ask yourself this: Can you think of any realm where *listening to understand* from another's viewpoint would *not* help you be more effective? Roger, the insurance company executive, said, "I have always considered empathy to be a cornerstone in developing good personal relationships, be they business, family, close friends, or whatever. You know, it just dawned on me, I don't have any close friends who are not empathetic. Over the years there were a few individuals, not a whole lot, that I couldn't stand and now I can see why. They were totally without empathy. Too bad, we each lost out."

Alice, a forty-six-year-old business consultant, wife, and mother, says, "It's *being there* for you, offering *emotional presence*—not *fixing* but letting you be *who* you are and *where* you are." She sees this need especially in her teenagers, who seem to want only that she listen and understand, without giving advice—unless they ask for it.

In my volunteer work teaching English to recent immigrants, I've found the more I understand my students' experience, struggles, and feelings about moving to this new and confusing culture, the more comfortable they seem in the classroom. And the more I treasure, love, and accept them. *Don't we all want to be understood?*

Here are a few things to think about, both in your work and personal life:

- The more you *listen to understand*, the more you will know how a person feels, and why he or she feels that way, and thus, the more you will appreciate, accept, and care about that person.

- Empathy leads to fuller, deeper, richer relationships.

- Empathy not only changes the dynamics in a relationship; *it changes the people in that relationship*, for a caring relationship helps us grow.

- When people feel understood and accepted, they feel free to drop defensive, judgmental, critical behavior.

Try this:

The next time you are talking with a friend, colleague, or loved one, listen carefully to their words *and feelings*; try to understand what they are saying—from their point of view. You might say, "Oh, I'll bet you felt proud," or whatever words show them you understand and empathize with them. Then notice how that person responds. You'll probably see their posture relaxing, a look of pleasure on their face, and warm feelings toward you.

Learning to sincerely empathize with others is one of the most important steps toward higher maturity. And it is a habit you can learn—it is *the power of you*.

Treat Feedback as a Precious Gift

40

*You must not fool yourself—
and you are the easiest
person to fool.*

—RICHARD FEYNMAN

We all have blind spots, things we do that get in our way, habits that we just don't see or know about. Yet everyone around us can see them, clearly. Think about the people you know well. Don't most of them sabotage themselves with some behavior of which they are unaware?

Because we're inside ourselves and can't see our own behavior as others can, the only way we can find out about our hindering hidden habits is through feedback from other people.

Fifty-one-year-old Judy is a good person, kind, bright and talented. But she talks too much. And listens too little. Both her work and her relationships are suffering, but she has no idea why. Her husband and friends keep trying to tell her, but she doesn't *hear* them. If Judy realized the value of feedback and *listened to discover*, she would hear her husband lament, "But you didn't give me a chance to tell you about it." She would see people fidgeting, glancing away, and looking bored as she monopolizes conversations. She could use that feedback as a gift to help her improve her relationships and her effectiveness. She would learn to talk less and listen more.

A surprising finding in my study of highly effective, ever-growing adults was that every one of these vital men and women makes a point of paying close attention to criticism, personal comments, and nonverbal signals from others. Rich, my ever-learning professor, said, "Even in harsh criticism there is always a germ of truth."

Warren Buffet said, "Success is not getting in our own way." One of the most important ways to become more vital and effective is finding a way to look into our blind spots, so we can become aware of our weaknesses and ways we are sabotaging ourselves, and do something about them. Only thus can we become our best selves.

When Marie finished her graduate work—an intense task for a single mother of two—she was packing her things in her student teacher office, preparing to move back home. Her office mate said, "But Marie, aren't you going to celebrate? You never celebrate." Driving home, Marie said to herself, "He's right, I don't celebrate." She does now.

The best way to learn about your blind spots is:

- Treat caring feedback and criticism as a precious gift. The people who care about you are trying to help.

- If you don't understand the feedback, ask softly—nondefensively—what they mean. Talk it over.

- Be aware that your first reaction will be denial. Because that behavior was hidden in your blind spot, you'll have trouble believing it—at first.

- Remember, unless you become aware of a problem, you can't correct it.

It will take you a while to welcome constructive criticism because most of us automatically resent and avoid it. It hurts. But once you get into the habit of listening to discover, you'll find it can help you live more effectively—and grow. Therein lies the power Robert Burns referred to when he wrote (interpreted):

O would some Power the gift give us
To see ourselves as others see us!
It would from many a blunder free us.

Dialogue—A Better Way to Communicate

41

The human mind, once stretched to a new idea, never goes back to its original dimensions.

—OLIVER WENDALL HOLMES

How well do we Americans communicate? Do we *really listen* to each other? The great physicist David Bohm, in his influential book *On Dialogue*, observed that in our competitive, fast-paced society we've lost the ability to *dialogue*. Instead we have *discussions*—a word with the same root as *percussion* and *concussion*. We bat ideas back and forth, as in Ping-Pong, competing to convince each other that our ideas and opinions are *right*. While the other is talking, rather than listening to understand his or her viewpoint, we plan our rebuttal. We don't *really* want to hear anything that may differ from our own ideas.

Four acquaintances were having dinner together and the topic turned to legalizing marijuana. George said, "Well, the money saved from law enforcement could be used for anti-drug education." Sally answered, "No! There is no excuse whatsoever for legalizing a drug!" Steve and Tess tried to offer their thoughts, but as they spoke Sally shook her head and frowned, refusing to listen to alternative opinions. In that discussion, no one was able to learn or to advance their understanding of the topic.

In contrast, the Greek root of *dialogue* means a free flow of meaning between people. We strive to learn each other's viewpoints, to acquire—together—new insights and higher levels of understanding. In a dialogue, everyone wins.

For instance, Ron and Deanna, parents of two young sons, joined a group of parents at a school meeting. Ron brought up their questions about spanking. Because each person had come in with firm opinions on the topic, everyone offered ideas about if, when, and why parents should or should not spank their children. All listened with interest and respect to each other's ideas, creating a vigorous, thoughtful, and *enlightening* dialogue. All went home feeling more knowledgeable about the topic, understanding that this question, like most others, is complex. There are no simple, clear-cut answers, and the best way to learn is to listen to all perspectives.

The great physicist Werner Heisenberg, known for his uncertainty principle, credits a lifetime of dialogues with brilliant scientists such as Pauli, Einstein, and Bohr with profoundly influencing and expanding his thinking. Though each had strong and sometimes opposing ideas, through dialogue all expanded their understanding of science. If each had dug in his heels and insisted he—and only he—had *the truth*, refusing to listen to and respect each other's ideas, all would have lost, as would the world.

Dialogue is like adding up the IQs of participants to produce a greater mind and insights than one alone could produce.

And take a moment to think about this: Because we identify with our opinions, we tend to vigorously defend them. But if your opinion is right, it doesn't need defending. And if it is wrong, what is the sense of defending it? Instead of arguing, try to listen to and understand the other person's reasons for thinking as they do. You'll be surprised at how much you can learn.

You can dialogue with one other person or with a group. A university social work class to which I introduced this concept was amazed at the results of their dialogue about capital punishment. Though their views differed wildly, later all agreed they'd never had such a productive and enlightening conversation about that topic, for until then none had ever *truly listened* to opposing ideas. All gained new insights and a deeper understanding of the issue.

Some basic principles of dialoguing:

- We pull back and observe our own reactions, realizing that when we feel discomfort or anger upon hearing ideas that conflict with ours, we are unconsciously trying to protect our pre-set ideas—and our egos.

- We mindfully try to drop our natural tendency to defend our beliefs, assumptions, and opinions, realizing that *only then* can we open up to new perspectives, understanding, and learning.

- We listen openly, respectfully, and attentively to each other's ideas, with the goal of understanding.

- We recognize that *together* we are more likely to acquire new insights, new ways of thinking, and higher levels of knowing.

Talk over the concept of dialoging with your friends, loved ones, and business associates. It's profoundly effective one-on-one or in groups. Most people, I've found, are not only receptive to the idea, but eager to learn about it and to try it.

Imagine living in a world where we all listen openly, respectfully, and attentively to each other's ideas, truly wanting to understand.

PART EIGHT

Friends and Lovers

Your First Three Minutes

42

*We awaken in others
the same attitude of mind
we hold toward them.*

—ELBERT HUBBARD

Years ago, my husband and I discovered something precious. We found that when we start the first few minutes of our day with sweetness and good humor, the rest of the day goes better. And so does our relationship. A good beginning sets the tone for the rest of the day. Even when, occasionally, we awaken feeling bombarded with problems, we make it a point to start out serenely and wait until later to talk about the negative stuff.

We honor the same ritual when we meet again at the end of the day. Instead of greeting each other with, "You won't believe what awful thing happened to me today," for the first few minutes we concentrate on being glad to see each other, and talk of positive things.

This same principle holds for the first three minutes you spend each day with anyone—friend, family, colleague, business associate, butcher or baker. *Your initial contact sets the tone for your time together.* With each person you meet, or talk with on the phone, start out with:

- A smile (have you noticed you can hear a smile in a voice on the phone?),

- Showing you're glad to talk with them (there are two kinds of people—those who, upon entering a room communicate, *Here I am!* and those who communicate, *There you are!*),

- Good humor,

- Careful listening,

- Genuine interest in what the other person has to say,

- A positive attitude (save the negatives to discuss later on, if necessary),

• Lively, pertinent conversation.

Try this little experiment: Next time you see someone you care about, concentrate on making your first three minutes together special, using the tips above. Notice how that person responds. Notice what happens to the quality of your time together.

Make the first three minute principle a habit in all your relationships. It works!

*There is
no such a thing
as too many hugs.*

R. Kirsten-Daiensai

Grow Your Romance 43

*The most important
thing in life is to learn
how to give out love,
and to let it come in.*

—MITCH ALBOM, FROM *TUESDAYS WITH MORRIE*

Love is the only rational act.

—ANONYMOUS

*The love we have in our youth is
superficial compared to the love that
an old man has for his old wife.*

—WILL DURANT ON HIS NINETIETH BIRTHDAY

A well-known author has a new book out about life after forty. Forget about romance, she advises. It's dead and gone once your relationship's initial sexual surge wears off and you settle into mundane, everyday life. "No," I thought. "not true!" There is *nothing* more romantic than love that survives dirty diapers and runny noses, rained-out soccer games and frantic runs to the emergency room. Study after study show that marriages tend to be happiest before the kids are born and after the kids leave home, for kids siphon our time and drain our energy. Romance, like a garden, flourishes best when we can give it our time, attention, and tender loving care.

When the kids move out, you can breathe a sigh of relief (and maybe shed a tender tear), turn to your mate and discover anew the joys of quiet time alone, touching and listening to one another, sharing ideas and dreams, laughing and playing—just the two of you. Finally you can sneak away for weekends alone in romantic hideaways, recreating that sensual serene intimacy for which we all long.

You may be thinking, "No, that can't happen to me—we don't have that kind of relationship." Even if your romance seems to have evaporated, if you love each other and care, it can be rekindled. And by romance I mean a deep, joyous, tender, caring love—a meeting of body and mind, spirit and soul.

A few years ago a cruise ship on the way to Alaska caught fire. One rescuer, wide-eyed, commented, "I've never seen such loving couples as those old people we helped into the lifeboats. They *adored* each other." And I've seen the same thing in many of our long-time-together friends—they're as much in love as any couple of any age. Maybe more.

When my friend Nina was widowed at forty-eight, she felt lonely, but found such pleasure in her career and community activities, good friends and grown children that her life felt full and satisfying. She dated often, but never fell in love—until after her seventy-second birthday. She met Mel, fell *definitely* in love, and married. On their first anniversary I called to congratulate them, and Nina confided, "Dottie, I've never been so happy or so much in love." Recently, on their twelfth anniversary, I called again. Nina said, "We're having such a ball together, and are more in love than ever. Every day we feel thankful, and lucky."

Is their happiness luck? I don't think so. They nurture and nourish their love, treating each other as we all want to be treated.

Here are fourteen ways to grow romance in your relationship:

1. *Make your relationship your first priority.* Love wilts when you put your work or your golf or your buddies first. An indifferent marriage, wrote Sarah Breathnach, "buries both partners alive with resentment."

2. On the other hand, *don't suffocate your partner.* For a full rich marriage, both partners must be fully functioning individuals in their own right. Two people clinging tightly to each other can scarcely walk together—they hobble each other. Two strong whole individuals walking freely, side-by-side, function best—together and individually.

3. *Competition* (except when playing) *is incompatible with a loving caring relationship.* Individuals perform, but teams win. When two people cooperate, combine their abilities and encourage one another, they create a synergistic, alive, vital partnership. They win.

4. *Laugh!* One of the most potent forces for keeping love alive—and for navigating the rough parts of life—is humor. And if you're not laughing enough now, don't worry. You can learn. Let yourself go. Laugh out loud! Chortle at funny movies and TV shows, giggle at your favorite comics. Laughing a lot can become a habit. And it's contagious. A woman prosecuting attorney was trying a case opposite a rude, arrogant defense attorney who resented women anywhere but in the bedroom. As the trial began, with pompous dignity he referred to her as Madam Prosecutrix. At first she was startled into silence, and then burst out laughing, as did the judge—and then the jury. From that point, the trial went smoothly. Try to displace anger with humor.

5. If you want to be loved, you must *be loveable*. And doesn't it make sense to be your most good-natured and thoughtful, loving and fun—*and* to look your best—for your beloved?

6. *Share the chores*. Real men *do* wash dishes, real women *do* mow lawns, and relationships where that happens are the happiest.

7. When you *help each other to grow*, your relationship grows. When over the years you treat your beloved with empathy and acceptance, consideration and encouragement, they grow and blossom. On the other hand, when we live with criticism, indifference, and disrespect, our soul withers and cries out in pain, as does our relationship. Sometimes we show the least amount of loving to the people we love the most.

8. And then there are the *guaranteed romance killers. Like nagging*. Insidiously and surely it undermines loving feelings. Instead of nagging, try writing a little Post-it reminder, start a to-do list, offer to do it together, or fire

up your creative juices to think up other alternatives. And don't forget humor!

9. *Saying "I told you so"* kills romance. (But sometimes you won't be able to resist *thinking* it!)

10. *Criticism* crushes love. Yes, it's easy and human to be irritated by some of your mate's habits. I'm lucky, Bill seldom criticizes. But I have a critical tendency that I'm working hard to conquer. What works for me is to ask myself if whatever is irritating me is important enough to be worth undermining our relationship and his self-confidence. And I remind myself that criticizing others only reflects my relationship with myself. Bill is who he is and he's wonderful, and I love his essence, so what right have I to expect him to change? I want to be loved and accepted *for the way I am*. Don't you?

11. *Never deliberately say anything to hurt your beloved*— even in the heat of a fight. Hurtful words imprint themselves on our psyche, never to be forgotten, and over time accumulate, eat away, and finally destroy lov-

ing feelings. Sticks and stones can break your bones, but words can break your heart.

12. *Communicate.* Talk things over and *listen*—you can't be a good communicator unless you're a good listener. And be sure you understand what the other means; too many disagreements stem from misinterpreting and misunderstanding. Check back, saying things like, "Are you saying…?" or "Do you mean…?" And share your ideas and dreams; as Lillian Hellman said, "People change and forget to tell each other."

13. *Lavishly show your love.* Bring your sweetheart coffee in bed. Cozy up on a couch and massage your darling's feet (do you know how sensuous that can be?). Hug lots, and even sneak a discreet squeeze around your honey's shoulders as you walk together down the street. When you go on a business trip, leave a love note on his or her pillow. And flirt! Have you ever watched long-time mates who've kept their romance alive? They flirt outrageously with each other—as if on a first date.

And say, "I love you" every chance you get. Whose soul isn't warmed by those words?

14. "Love cannot survive if you just give it scraps of yourself, scraps of your time, scraps of your thoughts," wrote Mary O'Hara. *Make time to be together*—to talk, to love, to laugh and play. Share precious moments—walk hand-in-hand on a misty morning, get creative together to cook a bodaciously succulent supper, snuggle up and listen to your favorite music. Plan romantic dates—like a quiet candle-lit dinner in a funky bistro, where instead of talking about the kids or work or your parents, you talk about ideas, each other, your dreams and goals and plans. And do sneak away for weekends in romantic hideaways.

Now try this:

 Take a moment to think about how you can make your relationship more romantic.

 Using the above fourteen points as triggers, jot down your ideas, and leave room to add more as they come to you.

Then, notice how your beloved responds, and how your relationship changes. (Love is an interactive process—when one person changes, the other must change, and…)

Happy loving!

Don't Be Afraid to Be Single

44

*People search for happiness outside
of themselves. That is a mistake.
Happiness is something you are,
it evolves from the way you think.*

—ANONYMOUS

*Every seed
in its sleep
awaits
the Light.*

—KIRSTEN-DAIENSAI

Before my research for this book I had the impression that single people are less happy with their lives, that their primary goal is to find a mate. How wrong I was! During my interviews of vital people, I found singles as satisfied and excited about their lives as those in relationships. Or more so. I had failed to see beyond my own long-time-married perspective.

So I investigated further, interviewing many more flourishing singles. What a revelation—and inspiration! When I asked them what they'd like to say to you readers who are single or could soon be, I heard echoes of the same themes, over and over.

Here is their message for you:

A chance to know your self. Everyone was adamant that the best part of being single is getting to know your self for the first time. Said thirty-seven-year-old Lisa, "You learn what makes you tick; it's painful at times, yet the more you learn, the happier you are. Finally I know my happiness comes from within; it's not dependent on another person. I feel independent, capable and strong. Part of that," she chuckled, "is because there's no one around to blame things on."

Kinne, forty-six, said, "You connect with your higher self. You find the power in yourself—you get whole. And when you're in balance, you attract people like that—the law of attraction."

Irene, fifty-nine, said, "All my life I'd felt obligated to parents, teachers, boss, husband, or kids. Now for the first time I can stand up and say, 'Here I am, this is me,' and it feels so good. I learned to build myself up as I built up my husband and children; I look in the mirror and remind myself of my strengths, and that I can accomplish anything I decide to do."

Give yourself time to adjust. When you're newly widowed or divorced, your transition can feel devastating, distressing, and depressing. Be patient with yourself; rebalancing takes time.

Being in a relationship is like two trees growing side-by-side, with roots tightly intertwining. Pulling apart, even to improve the health of each one, tears and ravages their roots. Each suffers and wilts, then slowly adjusts to its new unfettered environment, healing—and finally thriving, emerging stronger than ever before.

If you're used to thinking of yourself as part of a pair, shifting into your new role as a strong, centered, autonomous individual takes time and effort. Laura, fifty-six, confided, "After my husband died, it took me two years to heal. I found a counselor that helped, and wonderful self-help books. But from my crisis came growth; I feel stronger and happier now than ever before."

Ted, fifty-four and divorced eight years, said, "You can succumb to it (poor me) or you can *decide* to be happy. It's up to you. We're responsible. We can change our reality by our attitude—period. As Henry Ford said, 'Whether you think you can or think you can't, you're probably right.'"

Forgive. All agreed you can't heal unless you forget about past hurts—and forgive. Dwelling on negatives only drains your energy. It keeps you dependent. It weighs down your wings, dragging you down so you can't soar upward into a new life.

Develop friendships. Kinne said, "At first I thought, 'Hey, this is kind of fun; I can do whatever I want.' And then you get lonely. And then you realize you have friends. Now loneliness hits occasionally, but it can't touch the loneliness I felt married to the wrong person."

Ted told of the monk who, to achieve enlightenment, lived forty years in a cave. When he emerged, finally feeling successful, a young boy accidentally bumped into him and the monk shouted furiously at the child. He didn't understand that being enlightened also involves understanding and interacting successfully with other people.

As Henry Thoreau wrote, "Birds never sing in caves." To live fully, it's important to develop good friendships. Darlene, fifty-three, suggested, "Be friendly. Be direct with people. Tell them where you're coming from. And build friendships with both men and women; we need both perspectives." Most important, remember that to *have* a friend, you need to *be* a friend (see chapter 45).

"Don't limit your dating to potential lovers or soul mates. View it as making new friends; wonderful friends make life worthwhile," said Betsy. "If romance follows, fine. Aren't the best marriages based on a strong friendship?"

"And your married friends won't drop you when you become single," Sheryl said, "if you make it absolutely clear you *do not* and *will not* flirt with husbands—period!"

Lisa agreed, adding, "Flirting with a friend's husband is a good way to lose a lifelong friend for the sake of a short-term ego boost."

Get involved. All agreed that you can't be lonely when you're actively involved in life around you. Focus your energy on activities you love. Go places where compatible people go. Annie got involved in her community's little theater and through that developed a wide circle of stimulating friends. Others suggested starting a book or investment club, volunteering, or joining a health club that attracts interesting people.

"Every experience is an opportunity. You have to live life in the present, with full intensity—hear it, see it, feel it, smell it, taste it," said Lisa. "Be open. Going alone to new places or joining new groups can feel scary at first, but remember everyone there probably felt the same way at first. And soon you get over that fear and look forward to your next adventure."

Spirit allies. One surprise was that most of these vital men and women feel a loving, guiding, supporting presence watching over them. Depending upon their religion or philosophy, they call it God, spirit ally, or guardian angel. "Guardian angels can't come into our lives unless we ask them," said Ted. "You're never alone once you realize there's invisible help there. It's a comforting thing, a sense."

Love that freedom. And all covet their newfound freedom, to the point, said Irene, that "When a man gets serious, I lose interest. Some of my widowed friends feel guilty because they're enjoying their freedom so much. I'd love to find a soul mate some day, but I'm not willing to put my life on hold until then." Most of the singles agreed.

Love the solitude. Laura loves having time for her career and personal interests, confessing, "I couldn't do all this if I were married. And how I love my solitude! Though I'm a strong extravert, I cherish and guard my alone times. I'm embarrassed to admit that I sometimes resent it when someone stops by."

I wondered if attached people should listen carefully here, for every single person talked about loving their times of solitude. Do we grant each other enough personal space, enough quiet alone time?

Happiness is something you are. It turns out that we can be as happy single as in a relationship. The point is, happiness is a state of mind. It comes from within. And it doesn't happen by itself. It involves deciding to be happy and whole, and taking the necessary steps to get there. It involves risking to blossom.

Jot down:
- Brainstorming, list all the elements of your life for which you're thankful.
- Next, list other things you would like to have included in your life.

- For each thing you'd like to include in your life, write down all the ways you can think of to achieve it—letting yourself be wildly creative.

When would you like to begin? How about now? And enjoy the process!

LOVE HEALS

KIRSTEN DAIENSAI

Enjoy, Enjoy
For Life is Given to Us
Only
Moment by Moment

R. Kirsten-Daiensai

Real Friends
Fluff Your Aura

45

*Good friendships are fragile things
and require as much care as other
fragile and precious things.*

—RANDOLPH BOURNE

For decades the late Joshua Green stood as the pillar of business and society in Seattle—a symbol of integrity and accomplishment. His credo for success was, "Choose for friends and business associates only people of strong and good character." I've since discovered that was just about the most valuable advice I've ever had.

An old Hindu proverb says, "A man becomes like those whose society he loves." Since you are strongly influenced by those with whom you spend your time, doesn't it make sense to choose your friends and associates with care? Warren Buffett agrees, "I don't interact with people I don't like or admire. That's the key. It's like marrying."

Character surrounds itself with character.

Throughout our lives friendships become more precious and important—so much so that people with strong good friendships live longer, happier, and more active lives.

But good friendships don't just happen. To *have* a good friendship you must *be* a good friend. I truly enjoyed one of my graduate school friends; she was bright, witty, and fun. But this woman with so many positive attributes was almost totally self-centered and inconsiderate. Once we agreed to meet at a theater for a play. She never showed up. When I called, she said she changed her mind and decided not to go—but she never called to let *me* know. That type of incident happened over and over, until it was time to drop that friend. But still, I was sorry.

As with my school friend, some people will feel toxic to you. Then is the time to weigh whether it is wise to continue that friendship. Picture a balance scale, one side representing the positives in your friendship, the other side the negatives. If the positives outweigh the negatives, keep right on treasuring that friend. But when the negatives tip the scale, you may want to reconsider. If your friend is thoughtless, overly critical, dishonest, or a negative influence on you, it may be time to let go.

Or you may choose to back off and have an arms-length relationship. Not everybody has to be a bosom pal.

Another way to think about your friends is to ask yourself if they are balcony friends or basement friends. Balcony friends stand in the balcony applauding you, and cheering you on. They stimulate you to do your best and to feel good about yourself and to grow. They appreciate you for who you are, encourage you in your goals, stimulate your thinking, help you smile inside and out, and make you laugh. They add pleasure, beauty, and richness to your life. They deepen your spirit.

Basement friends crouch in the basement and try to pull you down with them. They corrode your spirit.

Make sure you are a balcony friend to those you care about.

But remember:

- We grow by being around people who are different from us. *If we surround ourselves with people who think and do exactly like us, we'll soon grow dull. Love your friends for their uniqueness.*

- Everyone has faults. *If we demand faultless friends, we'll remain friendless.*

If you have let a friendship develop frayed edges, perhaps through a disagreement or misunderstanding or unintentional neglect, and that friend is someone you treasure, work on mending your relationship.

But don't put energy into a relationship you don't want to grow. Let it go. Save your energy to nurture your precious friendships—with thoughtfulness and caring, humor and good times, appreciation and acceptance.

Real friends fluff each other's auras.

PART NINE

And Finally...

How Do You Know If You're Growing? 46

The only way to climb the highest mountain is one step at a time.

—ANONYMOUS

Remember Katie, my tousle-haired friend you read about in the first chapter, the one who dreaded aging and spurred me to write this book? As I was writing, we continued our walks, and talked about each chapter as it took shape.

Gradually, I noticed her attitude toward aging changed. And so too did Katie. One day she confided, "Before I felt like a cork held under. Finally, I've popped to the surface and everything looks different. I'm seeing my life in terms of opportunities instead of obstacles."

"I know I'm growing when I go back and read some of the first chapters in your book, and understand them for the first time. Now I see what T.S. Eliot was talking about when he wrote,

We shall not cease from exploration
And the end of all our exploring
Will be to arrive where we started
And know the place for the first time.

Betsy, who's been reading drafts of this book while at the same time going through a painful divorce, said, "With the stress I'm going through now, sometimes I feel as if I'm slipping backwards. Then I work hard on moving forward again, to let go of the pain and sadness and replace it with meaningful involvements and thoughts. Overall, I know I'm growing during this process."

When we choose to grow, we proceed not in a straight line but like a yo-yo being carried upstairs—up and down and around, all the while following an upward trajectory.

And when faced with a crisis, like Betsy we tend to slide back. But we *do* find our path again, often stronger and more energetic than ever—for it's the challenges we face that stimulate our growth. No pain, no gain.

And it's important for you to remember—each of us is unique. Thus we must each find and follow our own path, a way that belongs to no other.

Ron feels as if he's growing, for in the past, while driving to work on packed freeways, he always reacted angrily when another driver cut him off or drove irresponsibly. He'd arrive at work irritable and exhausted. Finally he decided to take control of his reactions, to turn his commute into a pleasurable interlude. Now he relaxes, flows along with traffic in the center lane, and listens to music. When another driver misbehaves he lets it go, thinking, "That's his problem, not mine."

My husband, who read every chapter as I wrote it, feels he's growing because he doesn't get so "bent out of shape" when projects get hung up in red tape. "Now I can roll with it, do what I can, flow with it—without anger—if there's no other way. And also, the power of empathy is so much clearer to me now."

You know you are growing when:

- You feel a deeper sense of meaning and purpose in your life—a reason for being.

- You get a sense of who you are, that you are unique, and that being yourself is just fine.

- And because you're OK the way you are, you realize you don't need to compete with anyone.

- You're more able to forgive and forget—with generosity of spirit toward yourself and others.

- You realize you're less self-absorbed so more able to connect with others and with life around you. You're feeling like a nicer person.

- You feel wiser, with a deeper understanding of life and people. A big part of that is seeing connections and interactions, how people and things affect each other.

- You become androgynous, meaning you're comfortable letting your masculine and feminine sides emerge to achieve a healthy balance. For instance, if you're a man you would feel comfortable writing poetry or learning to cook, and if a woman you might take up furniture building or fly fishing.

- You're more willing to take a chance, even risking failure or embarrassment, rather than to let go of a dream.

- When you feel mental dissonance, instead of stuffing it you look for what's not right and do something about it.

- You have more of a sense of control over you life, and realize things are working better for you because of it.

- Just as with getting more physically fit, when you're growing you feel more alive, energetic, and excited about life—and you experience more peace of mind.

- You're more accepting of other people, realizing we're all human and no one is perfect and most of us are doing our best—and viva la difference!

• You experience more precious moments, peak experiences when you feel infused with joy—and time stands still.

How about you? Which items resonate with you? In what ways do you feel as if you're becoming your very best self?

Inventory your thoughts:

1. Sit back and think for a while about ways you feel you've grown. Jot them down—and date it.

2. Next, jog your memory by reviewing relevant chapters in this book and write down the ways you'd like to continue growing. *Remember, personal growth is not a destination—it's a lifelong journey.*

3. When you've finished your lists, keep them in a place where you can go back every six months to reread and add to them, recording and dating your new insights and goals.

4. Over time you may want to reread some chapters in this book to see if they've taken on new meaning for you.

As I wrote this book, I began to feel a real connection with you, the reader. I care about you and would truly love to hear how you're doing with these ideas.

Please, enjoy your journey.

SEND ME YOUR IDEAS AND STORIES

I would love to hear your ideas and stories about ways you've found to keep on growing. Please write me at:

Lowell Leigh Books
27175 S.E. 27th Street
Sammamish, WA 98075

If you'd like a response, please enclose an SASE.

Or email me at DottieB@adultgrowth.com

SUGGESTED READING

Covey, Stephen R. *The Seven Habits of Highly Effective People: Powerful Lessons in Personal Change.* New York: Simon & Schuster, Inc., 1989.

DeAngelis, Barbara, Ph.D. *Are You The One For Me? Knowing Who's Right and Avoiding Who's Wrong.* New York: Delacorte Press, 1992.

————. *Real Moments.* New York: Delacorte Press, 1994.

Gawain, Shakti. *Meditations: Creative Visualization and Meditation Exercises to Enrich Your Life.* Novato, CA: New World Library, 1991.

Glass, Lillian, Ph.D. *Attracting Terrific People: How to Find—and Keep—the People Who Bring Your Life Joy.* New York: St. Martin's Press, 1997.

Goleman, Daniel, Ph.D. *Emotional Intelligence: Why It Can Matter More than IQ.* New York: Bantam Books, 1995.

Langer, Ellen J., Ph.D. *Mindfulness.* New York: Addison-Wesley, 1989.

Mahoney David, and Restak, Richard, M.D. *The Longevity Strategy: How to Live to 100 Using the Brain-Body Connection.* New York: John Wiley & Sons, Inc., 1998.

Nelson, Miriam E., Ph.D. with Wernick, Sarah, Ph.D. *Strong Women Stay Young.* New York: Bantam, 1997.

———. *Strong Women Stay Slim.* New York: Bantam, 1998.

Selye, Hans, M.D. *Stress Without Distress: How to Use Stress as a Positive Force to Achieve a Rewarding Life Style.* New York: New American Library, 1974.

Sokoloff, Dr. Arthur. *Life Without Stress: The Far Eastern Antidote to Tension and Anxiety.* New York: Broadway Books, 1997.

St. James, Elaine. *Simplify Your Life: 100 Ways to Slow Down and Enjoy the Things That Really Matter.* New York: Hyperion, 1994.

Tannen, Deborah, Ph.D. *That's Not What I Meant! How Conversational Style Makes or Breaks Relationships.* New York: Ballantine Books, 1986.

———. *You Just Don't Understand: Women and Men in Conversation.* New York: Morrow, 1990.

INDEX

Life Is an Attitude
How to Grow Forever Better
A Great Gift for Your Friends and Colleagues

Check Your Local Bookstore, Your Favorite Internet Bookstore, Or Order Here

❑ YES, I want _____ copies of *Life Is an Attitude* at $12.95 each, plus $2.50 shipping for the first book (and $0.75 for each additional book). Allow 7 to 10 days for delivery. (Canadian orders must be accompanied by a postal money order in U.S. funds.)

To Order:
Send your check and this form to:

Lowell Leigh Books
27175 S.E. 27th Street
Sammamish, WA 98075

My check or money order for $_____ is enclosed.
(Washington residents please add $1.11 per book sales tax.)

NAME_____

ORGANIZATION_____

ADDRESS_____

CITY/STATE/ZIP_____

PHONE_____

Ask About Our Volume Discounts